ing QTS
Extending Knowledge in Practice
Primary ICT

Achieving QTS
Extending Knowledge in Practice

Primary ICT

John Duffty

Learning Matters

For Siân and Rhys

First published in 2006 by Learning Matters Ltd.

British Library Cataloguing in Publication Data
A CIP record for this book is available from the British Library

ISBN-13: 978 1 84445 055 8
ISBN-10: 1 84445 055 4

Cover design by Topics – The Creative Partnership
Project management by Deer Park Productions, Tavistock
Typeset by PDQ Typesetting Ltd, Newcastle under Lyme
Printed and bound in Great Britain by Bell & Bain Ltd, Glasgow

Learning Matters Ltd
33 Southernhay East
Exeter EX1 1NX
Tel: 01392 215560
Email: info@learningmatters.co.uk
www.learningmatters.co.uk

CONTENTS

Introduction   1

PART 1: THE PLACE OF ICT IN SCHOOL   7

1 The place of ICT in school: planning and managing ICT   7

PART 2: EXPLORATION   15

2 Exploration in practice   15
3 ICT strategies: exploration   32

PART 3: TEXTUAL COMMUNICATION   45

4 Textual communication in practice   45
5 ICT strategies: textual communication   59

PART 4: MULTIMEDIA COMMUNICATION   72

6 Multimedia communication in practice   72
7 ICT strategies: multimedia communication   89

**PART 5: DEVELOPING IDEAS, MODIFYING AND
EVALUATING WORK**   105

8 Reviewing, modifying and evaluating in practice   105
9 ICT strategies: reviewing, modifying and evaluating work   118

PART 6: CONTROL TECHNOLOGY   130

10 Control technology in practice   130
11 ICT strategies: control technology   144

Index of teaching examples   159
Glossary   161
Index   165

ACKNOWLEDGEMENTS

The author's thanks go to the following companies and organisations for images reproduced in this book:

2simple, p53
Aspex Software, p111
BBC Science Clips, p100
BBC Wales, p78
Bedford Borough Council (Education Service for Bedford Museum and the Cecil
    Higgins Art Gallery), p94
Crocodile Clips, p77
d2 digital by design, p81
Data Harvest, p29, p139
Flexible Software Ltd, p34
Northumberland Local Authority, p154
Sherston Publishing Group, p79, p149
Softease Ltd, p48

Every effort has been made to contact copyright holders for permission to use the images within this book. In the unlikely event of any omission, this can be rectified in a subsequent edition by contacting the publishers (www.learningmatters.co.uk).

This book has been written to help you to develop your knowledge of the ICT curriculum and to translate that subject knowledge into effective teaching. Its aim is to enable you as a beginning teacher to extend your knowledge of ICT in a way in which will enable you to use it more actively in planning and implementing lessons. There are two related themes within this work; one is that the context in which ICT is developed should be both engaging and meaningful, the other is that the use of ICT should be seen as wholly cross-curricular. As Potter (2002) has indicated:

> *in an era in which the primary curriculum has been allowed to become atomised, ICT is uniquely positioned to make some of the connections again, allowing children to explore and learn in ways that most suit their curiosity and exploit their potential as problem solvers.* (Potter, 2002, p90)

Part I of the book describes the importance of ICT in today's primary curriculum, and offers an illustration of the way ICT is used in a 'typical' school.

The remaining sections of the book consist of paired chapters.

- **The first chapter in each part examines a number of practical examples drawn from school work, research and advice from experts and government bodies.**
- **The second chapter unpicks the curriculum expectations, describes a series of 'tools' which could be used to develop or enhance learning situations and discusses a range of professional issues.**

Part 2 identifies ways in which children can use ICT to develop their investigative and exploration skills, as well as developing effective learning practices. Part 3 highlights the importance of using ICT to develop children's communication skills when working with text. This is one of the most recognisable forms of ways in which ICT assists learning. However, with the advances in technology, children and young learners are becoming well versed in visual literacy, and the notion of movie films, cinematography and multimedia communication. As a result of this, some forms of written communication may be superseded by the use of multimedia. This is discussed in Part 4.

The importance of reviewing, modifying and evaluating work is illustrated in Part 5; clearly there is much overlap. When children are working with any aspect of ICT there needs to be some element of reviewing and evaluating. It is treated as a separate section here, simply as a way of emphasising its importance and as a means of clarifying the strategies that can be used. The notion of ongoing review and evaluation is a key component when working with control technology. This is explored in Part 6, which also illustrates and discusses the important development and learning opportunities to be gained from working with control and modelling technology.

Throughout the chapters you will meet a number of **reflective** and **practical tasks**. These have been designed to enhance your understanding of the material and to help you to place the ideas and strategies into situations which are relevant to you. The reflective tasks indicate areas where you can reconsider the elements under discussion. Learning is more meaningful if it is active learning; by carrying out the reflective tasks you will be exploring and analysing the ideas in this book in a more purposeful way. This will assist you in becoming familiar with the necessary knowledge and understanding.

The practical tasks are again intended for you to interact with the material. They will usually ask you to do something: to make notes, to adjust your planning, to organise teaching in a particular way or to adapt an idea already given. Clearly, depending upon what stage you are at within your studies, not all of the practical tasks will be relevant to you. However, it will be useful to return to them at a later date to work on them when they are more applicable. The practical tasks should assist you in becoming familiar with the necessary skills.

As well as each of the chapters being closely linked to the Foundation Stage areas of learning (the examples given here will still be relevant to the new Early Years Foundation Stage) and the National Curriculum programmes of study (the knowledge, understanding and skills that children should be taught), you will notice that reference is made to the new Professional Standards for Qualified Teacher Status (QTS). Please note that only the draft standards were available at the time of this handbook going to press. Although we do not anticipate any changes being made, if there are minor amendments these will be put on the Learning Matters website information for this title (www.learningmatters.co.uk).

The draft standards for QTS are set out in three interrelated sections.

1. The first section of the QTS Standards describes the **Professional Characteristics/Qualities and Responsibilities**: this section sets out the personal qualities that teachers should possess in order to meet their responsibilities.

2. The second section of the QTS Standards identifies **Professional Knowledge and Understanding**: this section indicates the areas about which teachers should be well informed.

3. The final section of the QTS Standards describes the **Teaching, Learning and Assessing**: this section states what teachers should be able to do.

The major elements in this book are designed to offer tools and strategies for developing your own teaching practices with ICT. This directly relates to the Professional Knowledge and Understanding Standard.

For example, many of the chapters offer specific guidance and tools to enable you to do the following.

- **Develop your *knowledge and understanding of a range of teaching and learning strategies for their subjects, and know how to use and adapt them to meet the varied needs of learners.* (Q2.4)**

- *Know how to use skills in literacy, numeracy and information and communication technology (ICT) to underpin their teaching and support their wider professional activities.* (Q2.6)
- Develop *a working knowledge and understanding of statutory and non-statutory curricula and other current initiatives for the subjects they teach.* You will naturally need to become familiar with the ICT requirements within the National Curriculum (NC) and the guidance offered for the Foundation Stage (FS). (Q2.2)
- Identify the importance of assessment and have *a secure and up-to-date knowledge and understanding of the subjects/subject areas they teach in relation to the prior learning, levels of attainment, future progression and transition of learners.* (Q2.1)
- *Make appropriate use of a range of monitoring, assessment, recording and reporting strategies as a basis for discussion with learners, and provide them with accurate and constructive feedback on their attainment, progress and areas for development.* (Q3.4)
- Develop your ability to *reflect on the quality of their teaching and its impact on learners' progress and use the findings to inform their planning and classroom practice.* (Q3.4)

Practical task

Read the Professional Standards for QTS, listed below, and in relation to ICT identify any Standards you consider you have already met and those that you feel will be your priorities for development.

Qualified Teacher Status Standards

Q1. Professional Characteristics/Qualities and Responsibilities

Teachers with Qualified Teacher Status (QTS) possess the knowledge and skills essential for them to be effective classroom teachers. These capacities underpin all the other Standards.

Teachers with QTS should be able to:

Q1.1 Demonstrate that they have high expectations of, and establish respectful, trusting and constructive relationships with, all the learners they teach.

Q1.2 Support and, where appropriate, contribute to the policies and practices of their workplace and share in the collective responsibility for their implementation.

Q1.3 • Understand the contribution that they and other professional colleagues make to the level of learners' attainment and their well-being.
 • Understand and respect the contribution that parents and carers can make to the level of learners' attainment and their well-being.
 • Communicate effectively with all children, young people, parents and carers.

3

Q1.4 Demonstrate a commitment to reflect on and improve their own practice, and take progressively increasing responsibility for identifying and meeting their own continuing professional development (CPD) needs.

Q1.5 Identify and use opportunities to work with colleagues and, where appropriate manage them, in order to share and implement effective practice in the classroom.

Q1.6 Adopt an open, positive and constructively critical approach towards innovation.

Q2. Professional Knowledge and Understanding

Teachers with QTS possess the knowledge and skills essential for them to be effective classroom teachers. These capacities underpin all the other Standards.

Teachers with QTS should:

Q2.1 Have a secure and up-to-date knowledge and understanding of the subjects/ subject areas they teach in relation to the prior learning, levels of attainment, future progression and transition of learners.

Q2.2 Have a working knowledge and understanding of statutory and non-statutory curricula and other current initiatives for the subjects they teach.

Q2.3 Know the national and local assessment requirements and arrangements for their subjects, including those relating to public examinations and qualifications.

Q2.4 Have a knowledge and understanding of a range of teaching and learning strategies for their subjects, and know how to use and adapt them to meet the varied needs of learners.

Q2.5 • Understand how the progress and well-being of learners are affected by a range of influences and use this knowledge to inform their teaching and to support learners effectively.
• Be aware of current legislation concerning the safeguarding and promotion of the welfare of children and young people.

Q2.6 Know how to use skills in literacy, numeracy and information and communication technology (ICT) to underpin their teaching and support their wider professional activities.

Q2.7 • Understand their responsibility to make effective provision for all learners and take active and practical account of the principles of equality, inclusion and diversity in their teaching.
• Know and understand the roles of colleagues and other professionals who have specific responsibilities for learners who are gifted and talented or who have other special learning needs.

Q3. Teaching, learning and assessing

Teachers with QTS possess the knowledge and skills essential for them to be effective classroom teachers. These capacities underpin all the other Standards.

Teachers with QTS should:

Q3.1 • Work collaboratively with colleagues as appropriate to assess the learning needs of all those they teach and set them appropriate learning objectives and targets.
- Work effectively as a team member in making a positive contribution to learners' attainment and their enjoyment of learning.
- Ensure that colleagues working with them in the classroom are appropriately involved in formulating lesson objectives and agreeing the role(s) they are expected to fulfil.

Q3.2 • Establish a purposeful learning environment where learners feel safe and secure and confident.
- Build constructive relationships and have high expectations of learners' behaviour.
- Establish a clear framework for classroom discipline to manage learners' behaviour constructively and promote self-control and independence.

Q3.3 • Plan lessons and sequences of lessons for the short, medium and long term. Teach well-organised lessons and sequences of lessons, informed by a sound and secure base of subject knowledge.
- Use a range of teaching strategies and resources to enable all learners to learn and make progress.
- Evaluate the impact of their teaching on learners' progress and adjust their practice where necessary.
- Identify and implement a range of suitable opportunities for learners to develop their literacy, numeracy and information and communications technology skills.

Q3.4 • Make appropriate use of a range of monitoring, assessment, recording and reporting strategies as a basis for discussion with learners, and provide them with accurate and constructive feedback on their attainment, progress and areas for development.
- Communicate this information succinctly to parents, carers and colleagues. Reflect on the quality of their teaching and its impact on learners' progress and use the findings to inform their planning and classroom practice.

Q3.5 Enable learners to:
- reflect on their learning;
- identify the progress they have made;
- identify their emerging learning needs;
- become successful, independent learners.

References

Potter, J. (2002) *PGCE professional workbook: Primary ICT.* Exeter: Learning Matters. Further details are available from: www.learningmatters.co.uk.

Qualified Teacher Status (QTS) is the accreditation that enables you to teach in state-maintained and special schools in England and Wales. Further details concerning QTS and the Standards can be obtained from: www.tda.gov.uk.

PART 1: THE PLACE OF ICT IN SCHOOL

1 THE PLACE OF ICT IN SCHOOL: PLANNING AND MANAGING ICT

Good teaching and effective learning have always been about making lessons interactive, relevant, memorable, fun ... the extraordinary pace of change in information and communication technologies is offering teachers, parents and pupils exciting new opportunities.
(DfEE, 2000, p5)

ICT has the capability to make a real difference to the learning which takes place, both in school and out of school. When pupils learn about ICT and when they learn with ICT they are being equipped to participate in a constantly developing world; a world where work and leisure time are continually adapting to keep in step with the progress of technology. Children are developing real, transferable life skills through their use of ICT. Chiefly, the effective use of ICT enables pupils to:

- **access, select and interpret data quickly and easily;**
- **be creative and to take risks;**
- **build cross-curricular learning skills;**
- **communicate with others and present information in a range of ways;**
- **develop the skills to select and use information in a discriminating, purposeful way;**
- **increase their confidence and independence;**
- **model, predict and hypothesise;**
- **review, modify and evaluate their work to improve the quality;**
- **sort and process data efficiently.**

Reflective task

The above bullet pointed list is in alphabetical order. Consider for a moment the features described. If you were to place them in order of importance, which would be your first choice? Which seems to be the least important?

There is no 'correct' order to the importance of the factors listed above, and your priorities may change for children in different year groups, for children with particular special needs and for those of differing ability levels.

It is clear that ICT has an important part to play in the education of children, but how does this use of ICT manifest in practical terms? Over the course of your training you will be working in a number of schools and educational settings, you will work with pupils from a range of year groups and key stages, you will have opportunities to see how learning and teaching with ICT is implemented and organised. The next section describes what you would find in a 'typical' primary school.

What to expect in a school situation

What kind of things can you expect with ICT when you are in a school? Remembering that every school or setting will be unique, this section offers some general answers.

Resources

As well as computers (or laptops) and internet access, most schools will have some or all of the following.

Table 1.1 Typical resources

Hardware	Software
• calculators	• clip art collection
• colour printers	• control programme
• concept keyboards	• database programmes
• control units	• desktop publishing applications
• data projectors	• image editing software
• digital cameras	• multimedia authoring
• digital audio recorders	• music composition packages
• electronic keyboards	• painting/drawing software
• floor robots	• simulations
• interactive white boards	• spreadsheets
• listening centres	• subject specific CD-ROMs
• monitoring sensors	• web authoring application
• overhead projectors	• word processing applications
• photocopiers	
• scanners	
• television	
• video cameras	
• video recorders	

Practical task

On your next school placement ask the class teacher or ICT subject leader for a list of the school's hardware and software. Use this list to inform your planning and teaching.

Organisation of the resources

As ICT development and provision have grown within primary schools, many teachers have adopted different approaches to that provision. Here are some organisational models you are likely to meet.

- *Classroom provision* – a small number of machines are used within the classroom setting.
- *Computer suite* – a range of computers assembled in one dedicated teaching space.

- *Clusters* – a small group, or cluster, of computers in areas close to the classroom or teaching space.
- *Mobile computing* – a class 'set' of notebook or laptop machines are brought to the pupils rather than the pupils having to go to them.

Some of these organisational models may be the result of space or financial constraints, or they may be adopted because they suit the needs and abilities of the staff and the children. Many schools employ a combination of these models: using a computer suite to boost children's basic skills in conjunction with maintaining an ICT presence in the classroom. This enables the children to use the classroom machines to continue learning between sessions in a suite.

CLASSROOM PROVISION
With the single computer in a classroom model, many teachers adopt the following organisational and pedagogical strategies as appropriate to the activity.

- Identifying clear learning intentions in planning.
- Planning short, timed, tightly focused activities.
- Planning activities across a number of sessions to allow sufficient time for all pupils to take part.
- Using a range of effective organisational strategies (whole class, group or individual) to allow completion of task without further teacher intervention.
- Organising the pupils to working individually, in pairs, or in small groups.
- Organising the room so that when two or three children work together there is space for essential collaboration and discussion to take place.
- Dividing larger projects into clear units with different groups or individuals taking on responsibility for specific parts.
- Making sure all pupils understand what to do if they experience a problem.
- Maintaining careful records to ensure all pupils have equal access.
- Setting appropriate targets for individual pupils.
- Ensuring there are appropriate opportunities for work to be printed, demonstrated, 'performed' or published on the school web site.

A SUITE OR CLUSTER OF MACHINES
The computer suite or small cluster of machines also has great benefits. Having a regular timetabled session means that teachers can do the following.

- Promote good practice to a larger audience.
- Reduce the need to repeat teaching points.
- Offer the pupils opportunities to all work on the same activity or topic area simultaneously.
- Observe children shortly after they have begun working on the computer so early intervention is possible.
- Use discussion and open-ended questioning to draw out what children have 'really learnt' about ICT.

Many of the same principles from the previous section apply in computer suites or cluster areas. However, working with a class or large group demands a range of organisational strategies.

- Pupils are easily distracted by computer screens around them, so clear rules are important.
- It is often necessary to have support from other staff.
- Find the best place to group children if lengthy explanations are needed.
- Keep children's attention by turning off the monitors when addressing the whole class.
- Provide 'help' cards for any new piece of software, the cards could be differentiated in the amount of help they deliver or in the way they are presented (text or pictures).

In computer suite areas, whole class demonstrations are still important. They should take place so that the pupils are clear what they are doing; however, these introductory elements should be kept brief so that the pupils can make effective use of their 'hands-on' opportunities.

Practical task

Before working with any children in a networked suite, discuss the procedures with your class teacher or the subject leader for ICT. Be sure you understand the organisational procedures and strategies that have been used in the past. If there are specific procedures for logging on to the network, be sure you know what they are and where all the relevant software is located. (Make notes.)

MOBILE COMPUTING

Once the machines have been set up and arranged in the teaching space, the practicalities of working are similar to the computer suite, described above. However, there are a number of other issues to consider.

- Classroom tables and/or chairs may be a poor height for comfort.
- Ensure there is sufficient space on the tables for pupils to work comfortably with the equipment.
- Laptop keyboards are ergonomically unfriendly and, over long periods of time, can become uncomfortable to use.
- Laptop lids can be closed in order to gain full attention of the group.
- There are potential hazards with leads trailing across the classroom.
- Potential problems with poor battery life.
- Screen glare and the fragility of the machines.
- Ensure the pupils can see the screen and you.
- The classroom is often seen as a 'better environment' than the suite for delivering instruction. This is good since it may mean that pupils respond better to 'whole class' introductory comments. However, a negative factor is that it may encourage you to spend more time delivering and thus restrict the children's practical ICT work.

Planning for ICT

All schools must use the National Curriculum as a basis for their planning. Many will also use the Qualifications and Curriculum Agency (QCA) scheme of work for ICT. Where this scheme is used, it should be adapted to meet the needs of the children and the circumstances of the school.

Curriculum planning in ICT will usually be carried out in three phases (long-term, medium-term and short-term). The long-term plan identifies the ICT topics that the children study in each term. These plans will show how teaching units are distributed across the year groups, and how these fit together to ensure progression within the curriculum plan.

The medium-term plans may be based on the QCA Scheme, and will give details of each unit of work for each term. This planning will identify the key learning objectives for each unit of work and may stipulate the curriculum time that should be devoted to each element. Schools that have mixed-age classes may provide medium-term planning which offers a two-year cycle of work to ensure appropriate coverage of the National Curriculum without repeating topics. Schools will plan to offer opportunities for children of all abilities to develop their skills and knowledge in each unit, as well as building planned progression into the scheme so that the children are increasingly challenged as they move through the school.

Short-term planning will identify the specific learning intentions for each lesson. These will be informed by the medium-term planning and assessment information.

Practical task

In your next school placement, collect the long-term and medium-term planning from the subject leader for ICT or the class teacher. Ensure you use this to inform your planning and teaching, building on skills the pupils have already gained.

Cross-curricular links

ICT contributes to teaching and learning in all curriculum areas. Across the whole range of curriculum areas ICT impacts the children's learning. For example, graphics work links in closely with work in art, and work using databases supports work in mathematics, while CD ROMs and the internet prove very useful for research in humanities subjects. ICT enables children to present their information and conclusions in the most appropriate way.

ICT makes a contribution to the teaching of PSHE and citizenship as children learn to work together and collaborate effectively. They develop a sense of global citizenship by using the internet and email. Through the discussion of moral issues related to electronic communication, children develop a view about the use and misuse of ICT, and gain a knowledge and understanding of the interdependence of people around the world.

Many ICT activities help to develop children's mathematical skills. They use ICT in mathematics to collect data, make predictions, analyse results, and present information graphically. In English, through the development of keyboard skills and the use of word processors, children learn how to edit and revise text. They have opportunities to develop their writing skills by communicating with people over the internet, and are able to join in discussions with other children throughout the world through email. They learn how to improve the presentation of their work by using desk-top publishing software.

Introducing a task

As the aims of ICT are to equip children with the skills necessary to use technology to become independent learners, it is important that the teaching style is as active and practical as possible. There are times when children are given direct instruction on the correct use of hardware or software in 'skills' lessons; however, ICT capabilities are most often used to support teaching across the curriculum.

Whenever a new ICT activity or new piece of software is introduced it is preferable to start with a whole-class demonstration and discussion. This discussion element is important.

If ICT sessions are regular and consistently involve group and whole-class discussions they are more likely to increase the shared level of knowledge, and the children's levels of confidence. As a result of this, the children should develop a positive attitude towards computers and a belief that everyone, with practice, has the ability to become a confident and proficient user of technology.

STRATEGIES
- **Make the focus clear and share your learning intentions.**
- **Demonstrate, describe and model good use of ICT.**
- **Use a mixture of open and closed questioning to judge the level of the children's understanding.**
- **Give only a few instructions at one time ...**
- **... but, offer several demonstrations: some children may find it difficult following mouse movement on screen.**
- **Ensure the children know what to do, remind them of the important points.**
- **Support your instructions with key points on the board or around the room.**
- **Group similar ability children to generate purposeful discussion.**
- **Ensure there is a clear role when children are working together, and encourage different turns in those roles.**
- **Use off-site visits to draw attention to the use of ICT in the real world.**

The Foundation Stage

In the Foundation Stage ICT will be used as an integral part of the topic work covered throughout the year. The ICT aspects of the children's work will relate to the objectives set out in the Early Learning Goals (ELGs) which underpin the curriculum planning for children aged three to five. Children will have opportunities to see and use a range of ICT equipment; they will learn about how ICT is used in the world around them and begin to use ICT to find information and to communicate in a variety of ways.

Children with special educational needs

ICT will form part of the school curriculum policy to provide a broad and balanced education for all children. Schools should provide learning opportunities that are matched to the needs of all of the children, and when planning work in ICT, teachers will take into account the targets in the children's Individual Education Plans (IEPs). Provision should also be made for children with specific needs. It may be necessary to have special hardware or software for children with physical difficulties, such as hearing, sight or motor difficulties (see Chapter 3 for more information).

Assessment and recording

Teachers assess children's work in ICT by making judgements as they observe them during lessons. Pupils' progress will also be assessed at the end of each block of work. A class record may be kept in the teacher's Assessment Folder. When appropriate, pupils print out work, and this is usually kept in their ICT Folios. Each child in KSI and KS2 may have a Self Assessment Folio which allows them to record and monitor their own skill progression. When a child demonstrates their attainment of a new level statement, they could show the evidence to their teacher and tick off the relevant box (levels I – 5). Self Assessment Booklets are designed to give children more ownership of their learning.

Practical task

Some questions to think about when you are on your next school placement.

- *What is the school's ICT scheme of work like?*
- *Are relevant links with other subjects identified?*
- *What strategies have been/are used for direct teaching of ICT to children?*
- *How are Teaching Assistants used in the teaching of ICT?*
- *Where will paired or collaborative work be used?*
- *Is there a portfolio of work available as a benchmark to demonstrate the performance of children at different levels?*
- *How does the school ensure that teaching builds upon the skills, knowledge and understanding in ICT that the children have learnt previously?*
- *How does the school show the importance of ICT work?*
- *Do all children have the same opportunities to work with the full range of ICT tools and techniques?*
- *What provision is there for children with special educational needs, and those children who are identified as being gifted and talented?*
- *If individual children need specialist equipment, will they have to be shared around the school or can they be kept solely for personal use?*
- *What informs long-term and medium-term planning?*
- *What resources are available, in terms of hardware, software and staffing?*

- *Who is responsible for maintaining the learning resources?*
- *Are children supported by the display of prompt/help sheets in the computer suite/cluster/classroom?*
- *Does the school policy include health and safety and acceptable use of the internet and email?*
- *What provision is there to protect children from inappropriate materials on the internet?*

Planning and managing ICT:

a summary of key points

___ *ICT can make a difference to children's learning in a variety of important ways.*

___ *Schools vary in the range of ICT resources that they have available and in how these are organised across the accommodation.*

___ *You need to familiarise yourself with how schools plan for ICT in the long, medium and short terms, and where ICT can be used to support learning in other subjects.*

___ *This information can be used when you plan lessons, in introducing tasks, differentiating work for different groups of children, and in assessment and recording.*

References

DfEE (2000) *Towards the classroom of the future: ideas in action*. London: DfEE.

Further reading

Potter, F. and Darbyshire, C. (2004) *Understanding and teaching the ICT National Curriculum*. London: David Fulton. This book discusses all aspects of the ICT National Curriculum. It offers some practical examples of how to deliver the content.

PART 2: EXPLORATION

2 EXPLORATION IN PRACTICE

By the end of this chapter you should:

- understand how ICT can be used to extend and enhance children's natural desire to explore;
- be aware of how children can use ICT to support their learning across all subject areas;
- understand the importance of focused learning objectives;
- recognise the close links between specific ICT skills and scientific learning;
- be aware of the range of ways in which ICT can support subject learning;
- recognise that exploration can be encouraged through questioning and investigations.

Professional Standards for QTS
Q2.1, Q2.2, Q2.4, Q2.6, Q3.3

Links to the Foundation Stage Guidance and the National Curriculum

In the Foundation Stage children will find out about and identify the uses of everyday technology and use information communication technology and programmable toys to support their learning.

At Key Stage 1 children will be involved in gathering information from a variety of sources, entering and retrieving information (1a, 1b, 1c). They will also be working with a range of information to investigate the different ways it can be presented, exploring ICT tools and talking about the use of ICT both inside and outside school (5a, 5b, 5c).

At Key Stage 2 children will be discussing the kinds of information they need and how they can use it, selecting and preparing and interpreting information (1a, 1b, 1c). Children will work with a range of information to consider its characteristics and purposes, working with others to explore a variety of information sources and ICT tools, and investigating and comparing the uses of ICT inside and outside school (5a, 5b, 5c).

Introduction

All learning is about exploring and making connections. From the youngest age, children have an inbuilt curiosity and desire to find out. This chapter will focus on the ways in which ICT can be used to enhance this exploration from the Foundation Stage to Key Stage 2.

The Curriculum Guidance for the Foundation Stage makes it clear that all children need:

> *opportunities to gather information to satisfy their curiosity. They do this in many ways ... asking questions of adults, of each other and of themselves... by looking at books, using CD ROMs, audio and visual reference material, pictures, photographs, maps, artefacts and products, and by talking to visitors and making visits.*
>
> (QCA, 2000, p83)

Clearly ICT is a tool that can support this. When children are first introduced to technology, they are involved in finding out how it works and what it can do. A remote control car, CD players, telephones and video recorders are examples.

As children move through the Primary years, they should continue to use ICT to help them explore the world, and to enhance all their learning. For example: using cameras or sensor equipment children can explore environments or areas which without ICT would be difficult or impossible to access; simple spreadsheets enable children to consider 'what if' type questions; and CD ROMs offer quick, easy access to a comprehensive range of data. In this way, technology can be seen as an extension of the senses; as a way of expanding horizons and opening up new ways of experiencing; and therefore, new ways of teaching and learning.

This chapter will highlight some of the ways in which ICT can support and enhance 'exploration'. This will be considered in turn for the Foundation Stage, Key Stage 1 and Key Stage 2.

Foundation Stage

The Early Learning Goals make it clear that children should be involved in finding out about, and identifying, the ways in which everyday technology helps us. For ICT, there are two specific aspects to the Early Learning Goals. Firstly, practitioners need to give children opportunities to identify and find out about the uses of everyday technology. Secondly, children should use ICT to support their learning.

Identifying everyday technology

Children should have opportunities to observe and talk about the ways in which technology is used. Many practitioners have found it useful to help children to classify technological and electrical equipment into groups in the same way in which they might 'group' shapes or coloured objects. Some of the simplest classifications could be to think about equipment that (for example):

- **has switches to turn it on or off;**
- **helps us to communicate (telephones, photocopiers, computer systems);**
- **is plugged in and works with mains electricity;**
- **needs batteries.**

Using ICT to support children's learning

Within the Foundation Stage curriculum ICT should be used as a tool to support learning across all six areas of learning. The most effective way to do this is to integrate ICT into the daily routine of the setting. As a student teacher it is important to use a good range of ICT resources yourself; to become a 'role model' for the children.

Think also about the environment of the setting. It should be possible to place ICT equipment in role play areas. For example: play telephones, answering machines and cash registers, calculators, videos, toy microwaves, electronic timers and scales, stop watches, clocks, cassette recorders, digital voice recorders, old PDAs, laptops or class computers can all be used in home, office or shop area.

It is also a powerful strategy to make ICT part of child initiated tasks. It should be possible to provide a range of simple software or CD ROM packages for the children to choose from. Similarly, making programmable robots or remote control cars available on a regular basis will help the children to develop skills and identify uses for ICT.

Where possible, build in specific opportunities for children to use the photocopier or telephone as part of your teaching sessions.

Practical task

- *Look back over the strategies just discussed and identify the ones you feel would be most appropriate to adopt on your next teaching practice.*
- *What other strategies do you feel would be useful to adopt here?*
- *Make a note to discuss with your teacher mentor how they integrate ICT into the learning environment of their individual setting.*

The Stepping Stones and ELG within the Curriculum Guidance for the Foundation Stage indicate that children will be able to:

- **investigate objects and materials by using all of their senses as appropriate;**
- **find out about, and identify some features of, living things, objects and events they observe;**
- **look closely at similarities, differences, patterns and change;**
- **ask questions about why things happen and how things work.**

(QCA, 2000, pp86–99)

The vocabulary of these expectations emphasises children's involvement in investigating, identifying and asking questions.

It is useful to think of how young children make sense of the world: through using their senses and by investigating, identifying and asking questions. Therefore in order to help children to understand the role played by ICT, it is useful to involve them in thinking about how ICT equipment can be used to extend their senses and how it can offer a means of recording information. Some of the best examples come from the medical world: doctors use x-ray equipment to help them 'see' where their eyes cannot, and stethoscopes to hear what would otherwise be difficult to hear.

In a school setting, the use of digital cameras offers unique opportunities to enhance children's attention to visual detail. The following teaching example illustrates this, and draws links between ICT and mathematical development.

Teaching example 2.1

Reception
ICT learning intention: to learn that technology can help gather information; to use a digital camera.

Mathematical development learning intention: identify and name simple 2D shapes (squares, rectangles, circles, triangles) in the environment.

The reception class teacher took a group of six children around the outside of the school to explore the immediate environment. The children had a simple digital camera and the teacher helped and encouraged them to look for shapes around the school building. They took photographs of the different shapes they saw: the bricks, the windows, parts of the fence, lines on the playground and posters on the school notice board. When they returned to the classroom they worked with a Teaching Assistant to load the images onto the computer. The teacher then shared the pictures with the whole class and asked the children about the shapes they had seen. They discussed the shapes of the windows and other elements they had taken pictures of. The teacher also encouraged the children to talk about how the camera had helped because it made it easier to see and to talk about the shapes when they returned to the class.

As a follow up, the children used a drawing program to superimpose specific shapes, squares, rectangles, circles or triangles on the digital images they had captured.

This kind of lesson clearly met the mathematical learning intentions. It also enabled the teacher to promote the real advantages of using ICT; that it was an effective means of capturing images as a memory aid.

The Teaching example also illustrates how the children were given opportunities to develop ICT skills, such as:

- using a digital camera;
- manipulating images;
- using a simple drawing package;
- superimposing drawn shapes on digital images.

The children were also given opportunities to develop their knowledge and under-standing, in that they were encouraged to see that technology can help to:

- gather information;
- sort information;
- clarify thinking.

In actuality, although the children had opportunities to develop all of the areas above, the ICT focus of the session was on the three Knowledge and Understanding areas. The teacher considered the Skills to be a secondary issue. She was 'seeding' the skills; preparing the way for a future session where these would be more formally practised and consolidated.

Key Stage 1

Practical task

In your next teaching practice, use the table below to unpick a taught session in a similar way: identify the skills, and then the elements of knowledge and understanding the children had opportunities to develop. Next, highlight the elements that you had intended to be the main focus of the learning.

Skills	Knowledge and Understanding

It will be helpful to carry out this task for a number of your planned lessons. Then consider the areas you chose for the main focus: do they regularly fall into the Skills or the Knowledge and Understanding portion of the table? If so, is this deliberate? What amendments could you make to redress the balance?

ICT can enhance learning across the whole curriculum. However, when considering the ways in which ICT develops children's exploration and investigative skills, the most direct link is to the curriculum area of science. In the following Teaching example, a digital microscope is used by Year 1 children to enhance their study of minibeasts.

Teaching example 2.2

Year 1

ICT learning intention: to use a digital microscope to magnify, examine and capture still and moving images.

Science learning intention: to identify differences between, and make comparisons of, minibeasts.

The children in this Y1 class had been exploring the environment around the outside of their school. They had talked about the insects, beetles and spiders that lived in the school grounds. During an explorative walk they made a collection of some of these 'minibeasts' and examined them directly and then using a magnifying glass. The teacher helped them to safely take a small number of the minibeasts into the classroom where a digital microscope had been set up. With this the teacher and the children could examine the creatures in more detail. They set the magnification to 10x and projected the image of a beetle onto the white board. The whole class could clearly see and examine the beetle's head, body and legs. The teacher helped the children to take some still images and to record a brief piece of digital video. The beetle was then returned to the safety of its habitat outside. The class could continue to examine images of it, and even watch the way it moved.

Practical task

Read the Programme of Study (POS) for Key Stage 1 Science (Figure 2.1 opposite) and make a note of which science areas are directly supported by the use of ICT in the above Teaching example.

In the Knowledge and Understanding section, paragraph 2g makes direct reference to ICT; and within the Breadth of Study requirements, ICT is specifically referred to in paragraph Ic. However, ICT Knowledge, Understanding and Skills should be seen as being capable of supporting almost all of the sections of the science curriculum.

The ICT used in Teaching example 2.2 served two closely related purposes. The main focus of the session was for the children to use ICT to help them compare and examine minibeasts. However, as part of this work, the children were also involved in discussing the advantages that the technology provides; they were learning about and appreciating the power of ICT.

Reflective tasks

- *Look back at Teaching example 2.1, from the Foundation Stage section of this chapter. Can you see any similarities in the way in which the teacher's use of ICT served two purposes?*
- *Think about your most recent teaching practice and the times when you utilised ICT in your sessions. Were you able to engage the children in ways that enhanced their appreciation of the power of ICT beyond the practicalities of the teaching session itself?*

Knowledge, Skills and Understanding

Ideas and evidence in science
1. Pupils should be taught that it is important to collect evidence by making observations and measurements when trying to answer a question.

Investigative skills
2. Pupils should be taught to:
    a. ask questions (for example, 'How?', 'Why?', 'What will happen if...?') and decide how they might find answers to them;
    b. use first-hand experience and simple information sources to answer questions;
    c. think about what might happen before deciding what to do;
    d. recognise when a test or comparison is unfair.

    Obtaining and presenting evidence
    e. follow simple instructions to control the risks to themselves and to others;
    f. explore, using the senses of sight, hearing, smell, touch and taste as appropriate, and make and record observations and measurements;
    g. communicate what happened in a variety of ways, including using ICT (for example, in speech and writing, by drawings, tables, block graphs and pictograms).

    Considering evidence and evaluating
    h. make simple comparisons (for example, hand span, shoe size) and identify simple patterns or associations;
    i. compare what happened with what they expected would happen, and try to explain it, drawing on their knowledge and understanding;
    j. review their work and explain what they did to others.

Breadth of Study
1. During the key stage, pupils should be taught the Knowledge, Skills and Understanding through:
    a. a range of domestic and environmental contexts that are familiar and of interest to them;
    b. looking at the part science has played in the development of many useful things;
    c. using a range of sources of information and data, including ICT-based sources;
    d. using first-hand and secondary data to carry out a range of scientific investigations, including complete investigations.

2. During the key stage, pupils should be taught to:
    a. Use simple scientific language to communicate ideas and to name and describe living things, materials, phenomena and processes.

Health and safety
    b. recognise that there are hazards in living things, materials and physical processes, and assess risks and take action to reduce risks to themselves and others.

(Adapted from DfEE/QCA NC, 1999a, pp16–20)

Figure 2.1 Science Programme of Study (Key Stage I)

Practical task

Think of the ICT you have used and the techniques you have seen used in schools. Read the Programme of Study again and use the following table to note any software or ICT skills which you feel can support the scientific areas. It will be useful to return to this task at the end of the chapter.

Key Stage 1 Programme of Study for Science	Ways in which ICT can support scientific exploration
Data collection (1)	
Asking investigative questions (2a)	
Using simple information sources (2b)	
Exploring and recording observations and measurements (2f)	
Making simple comparisons (2h)	
Reviewing their work and explaining what they did to others (2j)	

As well as using technology to amplify or improve our senses, ICT can also be used to offer children a range of secondary information. CD ROM encyclopaedias, for example, can offer large quantities of data available in accessible formats. The navigation structure of some CD ROMs matches the navigation of a book, but the addition of images and the wealth of easily searched data are highly motivational for children. In the following Teaching example a Year 2 teacher used a Dorling Kindersley music CD ROM. This particular CD enabled children to research and investigate a range of musical instruments, they could locate information regarding the instruments' country of origin, musical family, the material they were made from and even hear the sounds they produced.

Teaching example 2.3

Year 2

ICT learning intention: to use the navigation and search features of a CD ROM encyclopaedia.

Music learning intention: to identify key features of a range of musical instruments.

As part of a musical project the children had worked with several instruments and were now using a DK musical encyclopaedia CD-ROM. The children worked in pairs to find out about different musical instruments, the type of instrument (woodwind, string) the material they were made from and their octave range. This information was collected on an A3 paper matrix.

	Type	Material	Octave range
Trumpet			
Violin			
Kettle drum			
Flute			

On the matrix the children wrote the information they found after searching the CD ROM. For some children it would have been appropriate for the whole task to have been enhanced with ICT. The matrix could have been a word-processed document or a classification and sorting program like 2connect. This would also have enabled some children to use 'cut and paste' techniques.

Note that the organisation gave the task a very good focus; the data collection matrix gave the children the freedom to explore the CD ROM to locate a range of information, but they were still constrained within the parameters the teacher had prepared.

Practical task

Can you develop another idea along these lines? Could the matrix be developed to give more freedom, or adapted to provide additional support? What other forms of data collection could be devised that gives the children freedom to explore while also providing a clear structure?

Have you found that the children you have worked with are able to classify or organise data effectively? If not, what other support could you offer to help them?

As well as CD ROMs, the internet can also offer a huge range of secondary data. However, there are specific issues that need to be considered when searching for information on the internet; these will be discussed in detail in Chapter 4.

Children who use CD ROM or internet-based information sources will be involved in navigating, locating, evaluating and presenting information. There are clear literacy links here as the children will be using and developing their comprehension skills.

Reflective task

Think back to any occasions where you have observed or supported children using secondary sources, such as CD ROM encyclopaedias. Were the children fully motivated and enthusiastic about the investigation? If not, what can be done to develop and maintain their motivation and engagement?

Key Stage 2

Within the focus of exploring and investigating, the Key Stage 2 Programme of Study for ICT indicates that children should:

1a) Talk about what information they need and how they can find and use it.
1b) Prepare information for development using ICT, including selecting suitable sources, finding information, classifying it and checking it for accuracy.
1c) Interpreting information, to check it is relevant and reasonable and to think about what might happen if there were any errors or omissions.
2c) Use simulations and explore models in order to answer 'what if' questions, to investigate and evaluate the effect of changing values and to identify patterns and relationships.

(Adapted from DfEE/QCA, 1999b, pp18–19)

The following Teaching examples illustrate how children were engaged in the exploration process, and how the elements of the POS were incorporated into the teaching and learning.

Teaching example 2.4

Year 3
ICT learning intention: to use a concept planning tool to organise and share information.

History learning intention: to identify the reasons why the Vikings invaded and settled in Britain.

Using the QCA history scheme, the teacher had arranged for the children to undertake a study of the Vikings in Britain (QCA Unit 6c). The children had spent several weeks investigating the Viking invasions. The teacher had planned this lesson as a way of assessing their understanding of the Viking period while introducing the 2connect software to the children. The children used written notes and project information they had created over the course of the project and, working in pairs, they produced electronic mind-maps using the software.

The children used 2connect, a concept mapping and planning tool to help them reframe and organise information. They also discussed the information they needed and organised it while working on a history project.

This session addressed POS Ia (*talk about what information they need…*) and POS Ib (*prepare information for development…*). The activity was designed to encourage collaborative learning; the children were paired to enable them to engage in discussion about the Vikings and the reasons for the invasion (Ia). This concept mapping software models the practice of creating mind-maps, or concept webs. The children were using it to sort and define their ideas as they produced the concept web to share with the rest of the class (Ib).

This Teaching example also illustrates that occasionally the most useful computer software is very flexible in nature. In this case the concept mapping software could be used to serve many different purposes; although the Teaching example had a history focus the software could equally well be used to support any area of the curriculum.

Teaching example 2.5

Year 5

ICT learning intention: to use a database program and to check specific information for accuracy and to correct any implausible data.

Geography learning intention: to use appropriate geographical vocabulary.

The class was preparing for a geographical project on rivers. For a later part of the project the teacher wanted the children to interpret data in a 'rivers' database. The teacher decided to prepare the children for that activity by giving them the opportunity of searching for and checking data in a smaller database. Some parts of the data, however, had been deliberately entered incorrectly, and the children were given the task of interrogating, checking and amending the spurious information.

As they progressed the teacher discussed the importance of entering data carefully. If spelling is inconsistent then searching a database will produce errors. Similarly, if certain database fields accept units in kilometres, then errors will occur if entries are made using metres or miles.

The accuracy and relevance of information is obviously important, and the teaching session had a specific ICT purpose. It was designed to address POS Ic (*interpreting information to check it is relevant and reasonable …*). The tight ICT focus on skills meant that, although the work was leading towards using a database as part of a geographical project, at this stage there was no more specific geographical learning intention.

This lesson idea was adapted from a 'short focused task' in the QCA Scheme of Work for ICT, Unit 5c (*evaluating information, checking accuracy and questioning plausibility*). The idea of the 'short focused task' is that it is skills based. The children have opportunities to become familiar with specific skills which they will then use independently during a later task.

Practical task

When planning ICT sessions for your next teaching practice, think of the intermediate steps that children may need to work through before attempting the learning intention you are preparing. If necessary, create 'short focused tasks' that will allow the children to practise some of the skills they will need, and lead them gently towards the final task you have prepared.

Teaching example 2.6

Year 6

ICT learning intention: to use formulae in a spreadsheet program to solve mathematical problems.

Mathematics learning intention: to approach and work through problem-solving tasks systematically.

In this Year 6 class the children had been using the Microsoft Excel spreadsheet program for data-handling processes. The children were already familiar with many basic Excel features and formulae. Now they were challenged to use their knowledge and skills to solve a range of number problems such as 'the sum of five consecutive odd numbers is 245. What are the numbers?' The challenge was to find an elegant way to work out the solution.

The children set about unpicking the problem and working with simple formulae. Some chose to work out rough ideas on paper first, while others began entering numbers and calculations into the spreadsheet immediately. At intervals the teacher stopped them to discuss their work so far and to share ideas.

After 15 minutes most children had worked through a solution. Some had worked methodically, using copy and paste to reproduce their formulae hundreds of times: producing a grid with hundreds of possible results, and one highlighting the correct one:

33	35	37	39	41		185
35	37	39	41	43		195
37	39	41	43	45		205
39	41	43	45	47		215
41	43	45	47	49		225
43	45	47	49	51		235
45	47	49	51	53		245
47	49	51	53	55		255
49	51	53	55	57		265
51	53	55	57	59		275

Other children had worked more creatively. They had used spreadsheet formulae but also added a dose of intuition to take a 'lateral' leap to the correct answer.

The teacher involved the children in discussions regarding the calculations and decisions they had made. The children were also keen to discuss the relative merits of the different approaches they had taken.

The general consensus was that either method (since they both provided correct answers) was effective. However, the first, more methodical, method was voted for as being more reliable.

The exploration of patterns and relationships is a key mathematical concept. This Teaching example was clearly designed to fulfil elements of POS 2c (use simulations and explore models ...). Once children are confident with spreadsheet modelling, this use of ICT permits children greater freedom with their mathematics. Effective use of computer modelling will allow children to:

- visualise mathematical concepts;
- work with realistic, 'real world' type, problems;
- analyse a problem in more creative ways.

The first and third points were highly relevant for this Teaching example. However, with data-handling processes the second point takes on much greater importance. The fact that children can use realistic numbers, whether for population, currency or distances to planets, makes the investigations more meaningful, and the use of ICT means that the more complex mathematical computations do not intrude on the creative thinking.

Practical task

When preparing sessions for your next school placement consider how you can:

- *assist children to visualise mathematical concepts;*
- *offer children the chance of working with real-life problems;*
- *promote the notion that creative solutions are effective.*

The science connection

As was discussed at the beginning of the Key Stage I section of this chapter, there is one curriculum area which forges clear links with exploration and ICT: science.

Scientific work utilises ICT to:

- model ideas;
- search for information;
- automatically collect information;
- handle data from experiments;
- present information and data.

There are clear correlations here with the Programme of Study (POS) for ICT.

Science and ICT are so closely linked that it is important to make the connections throughout the whole school. Teaching example 2.1 (the Reception class using digital images of the school environment) indicated that exploring and searching can be made easier with the uses of ICT. Similarly, Teaching example 2.2, where Year 1 children investigated minibeasts with a digital microscope, supported the link between technology and science.

As well as using digital images, one of the clearest scientific applications of ICT is data logging. This is when the computer automatically records information about the environment. There is a whole range of data logging equipment and sensors that can be utilised with a computer. Many of the sensors measure changes in the environment; this could be the temperature, the amount of light or sound. Some sensors however can also be used with control technology to permit the computer to control simple motor systems or robotic devices. This will be considered in more detail in Part 6: Control Technology.

Electronic data logging, or sensing equipment, is used to help record experimental results. This is usually data that would otherwise be difficult to collect. Reading of light or sound changes over a long period of time or in an inaccessible location. The ease of collecting data in this way can motivate children to be more scientific because the number of events collected can be larger than if collecting in person.

The following example demonstrates this well. The children had carried out a science investigation to find suitable insulating materials; they used simple data-logging equipment (EasySensor Q) to measure the changing temperature within containers of water.

Teaching example 2.7

Year 4
ICT learning intention: to use ICT data logging equipment to collect temperature data over a period of time.

Science learning intention: to use line graphs to show continuously changing data.

This science investigation grew out of a design technology challenge in which the teacher asked the children to create an efficient insulation cover for a coffee mug. The children discussed different materials and were encouraged to form a scientific investigation to test the insulating properties of the materials. They designed an experiment which involved four mugs filled with hot water and covered with four different 'test materials'. The children then intended to measure the temperature of the water at intervals in order to decide which material was the most effective insulator.

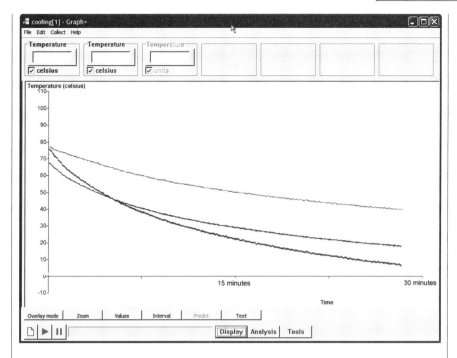

Figure 2.2 Line graph showing data

With the teacher's help, this direct measuring investigation was adapted to use data-logging equipment. The four mugs, each with hot water, were linked to four temperature sensors. The data-logging equipment and software were set up so that the sensors would automatically take a temperature measurement of each mug every two minutes. The software produced a series of line graphs indicating the changing temperature.

The temperature of the water in the mugs gradually dropped and the sensors recorded the activity for the next 90 minutes. While the children waited anxiously for the final results they prepared the next stage of their mug-insulation designs.

Under the teacher's guidance the children came to realise that measuring and record-ing temperatures 'by hand' over the course of an hour would have been tedious and impractical; it would also have introduced a range of possible errors. The automatic sensing equipment detected the temperature faithfully and automatically every two minutes. The data-logging software produce a range of line graphs which made the results clear. The children were also very pleased that this graphing element of the investigation had been completed automatically too.

Reflective task

Based on the description of this session do you feel that the science learning intention was achieved?

29

ICT has great potential to enthuse and motivate. When children interact with ICT they quickly learn that its ability to extend and enhance their senses can make them better explorers and investigators; they learn that technology is eternally patient and that its automatic functions can free them from tedious, repetitive tasks. These are significant learning intentions that children often address almost by accident. It is important that whenever children are engaged with using ICT they come away more involved in and knowing more about ICT than before.

Exploration in practice:

a summary of key points

- *ICT can provide a variety of ways for children to explore their environment and develop their investigative skills.*
- *ICT is a tool that can support learning in all six Foundation Stage areas of learning and in the full range of National Curriculum subjects.*
- *You need to be clear about what skills, knowledge and understanding you intend to be the focus of planned learning, for both ICT and the subject context of all activities.*
- *There are particularly close links between specific ICT skills and scientific learning.*

References

DfEE/QCA (1999a) *Science: the National Curriculum for England*. London: DfEE/QCA.

DfEE/QCA (1999b) *ICT: the National Curriculum for England*. London: DfEE/QCA.

OFSTED (2005) *Primary National Strategy: an evaluation of its impact in primary schools 2004/05*. London: HMSO.

QCA (1998) *A scheme of work for Key Stages 1and 2: information technology*. London: QCA Publications.

QCA (2000) *Curriculum guidance for the Foundation Stage*. London: QCA.

QCA (2005) *A curriculum for the future: subjects consider the challenge*. London: QCA.

Further reading

Potter, F and Darbyshire, C (2004) *Understanding and teaching the ICT National Curriculum*. London: David Fulton. This book discusses all aspects of the ICT National Curriculum, giving practical examples of how to deliver the content. The authors also discuss the difference between discrete teaching of ICT and the use of ICT to enhance teaching and learning in other subjects is outlined.

Resources

Mouse Music interactive CD ROM published by d2 digital by design
www.themouseclub.co.uk.

2connect from 2simple software www.2simpleshop.com.

EasySensor Q from Data Harvest www.data-harvest.co.uk.

3 ICT STRATEGIES: EXPLORATION

By the end of this chapter you should:

- **have knowledge and understanding of the requirements for 'exploration' within the ICT NC Programme of study and ICT within the Curriculum Guidance for the Foundation Stage;**
- **recognise the ways in which exploration strategies can be introduced and developed in the primary classroom;**
- **be able to reflect on your own practice and identify areas for development;**
- **be able to plan and organise learning in creative ways to enable children to find things out for themselves using ICT;**
- **be able to suggest ways of differentiating exploration activities with ICT;**
- **be aware of possible ways of assessing children's ICT capability;**
- **be able to Identify issues of health and safety in ICT.**

Professional Standards for QTS
Q2.1, Q2.2, Q2.4, Q2.6, Q3.3, Q3.4, Q3.5

Links to the Foundation Stage Guidance and the National Curriculum

In the Foundation Stage children will find out about and identify the uses of everyday technology and use information communication technology and programmable toys to support their learning.

At Key Stage 1 children will be involved in gathering information from a variety of sources, entering and retrieving information (Ia, Ib, Ic). They will also be working with a range of information to investigate the different ways it can be presented, exploring ICT tools and talking about the use of ICT both inside and outside school (5a, 5b, 5c).

At Key Stage 2 children will be discussing the kinds of information they need and how they can use it, selecting and preparing and interpreting information (Ia, Ib, Ic). Children will work with a range of information to consider its characteristics and purposes, working with others to explore a variety of information sources and ICT tools, and investigating and comparing the uses of ICT inside and outside school (5a, 5b, 5c).

> *With the increasing use of technology in all aspects of society, confident, creative and productive use of ICT is an essential skill for life. In this information age, effective learners and citizens need ICT skills. ICT enables us to find, explore, analyse, create, exchange and present information. A curriculum rich in ICT will help prepare learners to participate fully in a constantly changing world.* (QCA, 2005, p12)

Introduction

Chapter 2 considered a number of examples from schools where teachers were using ICT to help pupils develop their exploration skills. The intention of this chapter is to provide you with some tools and strategies to help you to develop your understanding of the demands of the NC in terms of exploration, to develop your own examples and to address a number of other issues.

Tools and strategies

Gathering information

Gathering information is the first aspect of the programme of study for Knowledge, Skills and Understanding in the National Curriculum (Key Stage 1: 1a/Key Stage 2: 1a). In order for pupils to be able to effectively develop understanding at Key Stage 1 they need to have had experience of investigating and exploring with ICT in the Foundation Stage.

Exploring is a central theme of ICT work within the early years. Children need opportunities to gather information and can do this through questioning. The Curriculum Guidance for the Foundation Stage also suggests that children should:

> have the opportunity to gather information by looking at books, using CD ROMs, audio and visual reference material, pictures, photographs, maps, artefacts and products and by talking to visitors and making visits. (QCA, 2000, p83)

Teaching example 2.1, in Chapter 2, focused on pupils' use of a digital camera to explore their local surroundings. Using the camera enabled the children to develop their ICT skills; specifically their ability to capture images using digital technology, and their knowledge and understanding of what ICT can do for them. In the session, the use of the camera was discussed as though it was being used as an extension of their natural sense of sight. As has been discussed, it is useful to consider ICT as an extension of the senses. For young children in particular, this makes the use of cameras, microphones and headphones more meaningful.

To take 'senses' in a literal fashion: children are expanding and developing their senses of sight and touch, etc. whenever they are working. They are doing this when their fingers interact with the keyboard or mouse and they begin to learn what the individual buttons can do. Most children quickly come to terms with the association between what they do with the mouse and what happens on screen, for example. This can also be linked to the holistic curriculum in that children are also developing their fine motor skills at the same time as exploring the ICT.

Another point which can be drawn from this example is allowing the children time to explore, and to form their own conclusions. In this way it is possible to deepen the children's enthusiasm and urge to experiment, while at the same time beginning to assess their understanding of the concepts they are meeting. It seems counter-intuitive, but it is important to resist the urge to 'teach', in the sense of 'telling' since doing this too early can stop children's natural exploratory sense. Pupils in an early years class, for example, experimenting with magnets, need opportunities to explore what they can do, opportunities to sense the wonder, the fun and excitement that these strange objects can create, and opportunities to talk about and share their ideas. Offering an explanation, a 'correct definition' of the material and what it does, can squash that sense of excitement and creativity. This notion of 'giving the game away' may in fact *limit the depth of children's learning* (QCA, 2000, p83). It seems only natural that as teachers we want to give information; to teach. However, this can prevent pupils from working through that 'eureka moment' and possibly delay the development of investigative skills.

Reflective task

Think about discussions you have had with pupils exploring a new concept; do you offer to teach before they have time to learn? If so, what strategies can you think of to support the children's investigations without over-teaching them?

A very effective ICT application for developing children's understanding of concepts is a branching database. These applications, sometimes referred to as 'decision trees', offer a clear way of sorting and classifying a set of objects. The pupils are encouraged to think deeply about the features of the set of objects in order to locate differences. These differences are then used to separate the set into two discrete groups. Each group is again subdivided by thinking of a characteristic. The subdivisions continue until all of the objects are sorted. The activity works well with real objects, but the ICT adds considerably in that it can instantly display the growing tree diagram and make the processes involved very clear to the pupils.

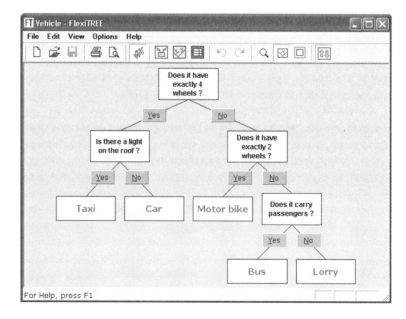

Figure 3.1. Flexitree image

The following demonstrates the power of utilising a branching database or decision tree software. The teacher was developing a theme on the topic of materials. The pupils had already carried out a number of investigations to determine the different properties of materials, they were familiar with a number of concepts, and the vocabulary: particularly opaque/translucent, magnetic/non-magnetic, porous/non-porous, natural/man-made. The teacher explained how the branching database worked using a range of data from the class. Together, they sorted a range of coloured shapes according to one criterion, and devised a single yes/no question that would describe the difference between the two groups: 'Is it red?' for example. The teacher demonstrated how this could be entered into the computer application (Flexitree, see Figure 3.1). When the simple demonstration tree had been completed the pupils were encouraged to use their existing knowledge of materials to create a branching database of their own.

The ability to identify important criteria, and describe similarities and differences are key information handling skills. When pupils are using branching database applications they are doing more than entering a series of facts and descriptions into a computer program, they are involved in classifying a range of objects and searching for, and asking, effective questions.

Reflective task

Consider the above description. What do you feel were the teacher's learning intentions for ICT? For science?

The National Council for Educational Technology (NCET, now known as Becta) suggested that when making a simple investigation, the following process takes place. Pupils should do the following.

Engage with the investigation. At the engagement stage it is important to provide a good context so that the pupils' interest and involvement in the task is clear. It is also important to define a clear purpose and decide what data to look at.

Gather information. When gathering information or data the children should be encouraged to find all possible avenues of gathering data and to freely explore it.

Make connections and ask questions. When the pupils are involved in making connections and asking questions they will be taking an inquisitive look at the organised data, asking purposeful questions and asking about relationships. It may also be necessary for them to begin sorting, classifying or browsing through the data.

Look for answers. The next step in the process is when the pupils begin looking for answers. Here they are involved in interrogating the data, looking for relationships/correlations and counter examples. It is also important that the pupils take part in discussing whether the answer is yes, no or unproven.

Interpret the information. At this stage in the process pupils will be adopting a sceptical view and questioning the validity of the finding. There will also be interpretation and explanation – from what to why.

Achieve an outcome. Lastly the pupils will have new knowledge and a deeper under-standing leading to further enquiry. Aspects of their ICT skills, knowledge and understanding should also have been developed (Adapted from NCET, 1995).

If we look again at one of the examples given in the previous chapter, the use of a digi-tal camera to help children to identify 2D shapes in the environment, we can begin to unpick the process of exploration that took place and also map the development of ICT understanding and skills (Table 3.1).

Table 3.1. Mapping understanding and skills

The exploration process	The activity	The development of ICT understanding and skills
Engage with the investigation process: 2D shapes are important	thinking and talking about 2D shapes	
Gather information about 2D shapes in the environment	exploring the school grounds taking photographs	• technology can help gather information • using digital camera
Making connections and asking questions about the types of shapes they have seen	sorting and discussing the images	• technology can help sort information • using images
Look for answers	looking for relationships between images – matching drawn shapes to those photographed	• technology can help clarify thinking • using drawing package • superimposing drawn shapes onto digital images
Interpret the information	discussing what they have found out about common 2D shapes	• technology helps to share images and information
Achieve an outcome	greater knowledge of 2D shapes in the environment	• the development of ICT skills and confidence

Of course, not all investigations start at the same place. If it is your learning intention for the pupils to 'interpret information', for example, then it would be useful to give them the information, the connections and the questions so that their learning (and the activity) is tightly focused.

Practical task

The next time you encourage pupils to explore avenues and discuss options, think about the above exploration process.

Write a plan that will enable the pupils to work through the appropriate phases of the process.

The **making connections and asking questions** part of the process is one of the most important and potentially creative phases. The 2connect software discussed in Chapter 2 is effective at encouraging pupils to see links and associations between elements. Branching database software is similarly effective at supporting pupils' questioning skills. The most powerful questions should lead to the most interesting enquiries. Many children, however, will need more support with their questioning skills. In this, we as teachers must play an important role.

Student teachers often choose closed, knowledge-based questions like *Who was Henry VIII's first wife?* because once the child responds, the next step is clear. If they have responded correctly then praise is administered, if they are incorrect then further support is necessary. The 'next step' is less clear cut with open-ended questions. However, open-ended questions are important tools. *What would happen if…? Why do you think that …? Can you find a way to …?* All encourage pupils to describe experiences, share what they have learnt and to consider future possibilities. When pupils are exploring databases, or using CD ROMs to locate information it is useful to plan ahead and be prepared with the kind of questions you expect them to use in order to locate the information. Direct, closed questions give pupils the chance to locate direct facts. Open-ended questions help them to think around the subject and the searches they carry out will be wider and, potentially, more purposeful. However, there may be more occasions when they achieve frustration rather than answers.

Practical task

On your next professional placement carefully consider the key questions you note on your lesson planning. Are they knowledge-based, closed questions or are they more reflective and open-ended like 'What would happen if…?'

Are the pupils asking purposeful and productive questions? If not, what strategies can you use to help them develop their skills?

If pupils are asking open-ended questions there is a greater risk of their being dissatisfied, or confused, by the information they find. What can you do to support them with this?

The exploration process has very clear links with science. As with all other areas it is important to embed ICT science techniques into science teaching and not as stand-alone ICT skills development. ICT should be seen as part of scientific enquiry. The Teaching example 2.2, in the previous chapter, described Year I children investigating minibeasts. They were using a digital microscope to help them see the minibeasts and were using elements of the exploration process described above to help them to identify some of the differences between the beetles and other minibeasts they had collected. They were using ICT to help them examine them and, since they could record the creatures' movements it was also possible to examine them in detail after they had been returned to the safety of their habitat. This clearly allowed the teacher to emphasise PSHE and ethical issues while permitting the pupils' curiosity and exploration to continue.

Entering, storing and retrieving information

Within the Foundation Stage pupils will have experience of entering information into a computer system. The storing and retrieving, however, will mainly be an automatic facility provided by the software. It is still important for them to realise that the commands they enter into a programmable toy are stored for a short time. In a similar way, the sounds they record onto a tape (or digital) recorder are stored and can be played back (retrieved) again at will.

The skills of entering, storing and retrieving information are key aspects of the programme of study for knowledge skills and understanding in the ICT National Curriculum (Key Stage 1: 1b, 1c/Key Stage 2: 1b, 1c). Initially, this may take the form of entering text information into a word-processor, or data into a prepared database.

Teaching example 2.5, in the previous chapter, described a session where pupils were involved in working with data on a rivers project. They were given a database containing multiple errors and were asked to correct and improve the data. This had a particular, tight focus, and the teacher had designed the session so that the pupils would be developing specific skills.

As the children gather independence with their uses of exploration, they should be becoming more responsible with their use of ICT. It is important that children are taught how to:

• **open and close programs;**
• **save and print their work;**
• **find, load and amend their work.**

Reflective task

What technical skills and ICT capabilities did the pupils at your last school have?

What specific opportunities could you plan to enable children to develop their technical capabilities?

Professional issues

Planning and organisation

The NC Programmes of study for ICT are the basis for planning, teaching and assessment. When planning for the use of ICT, it is important to have a clear understanding of the:

- **requirements of the National Curriculum;**
- **learning intentions for the ICT development;**
- **ICT skills which will be either supported or developed;**
- **assessment focus for the ICT capabilities, skills or techniques;**
- **learning intentions for the cross-curricular subject area;**
- **assessment focus for the cross-curricular subject area.**

The learning intentions are of paramount importance. For example, when children are exploring a CD ROM you need to consider whether the software fulfils your requirements. For example, does the CD ROM:

- **present pupils with a series of puzzles and linked activities like The Crystal Rainforest or Learning Ladder?**
- **simulate a reference book, like The Ultimate Human Body?**

If your learning intention concerns the development of thinking skills, then the first type of software matches the needs. However, if you are concerned with pupils using and developing comprehension skills, the second type (an electronic information book in which to look up answers to questions) will be the most suitable.

The facilities which are available will make clear demands on your organisation. Working with a class of children in a computer suite requires different management strategies from using a single machine in a classroom (as was discussed in Chapter 1). The pace and general nature of the work will also be different. Similarly, the amount of time children need to spend on an activity will depend upon their confidence with the software and the nature of the task. Short, ten-minute tasks can build confidence with programs and allow effective, well focused assessment strategies. For example, pupils may begin using word processing applications for short tasks such as writing their name, making labels, or adapting previously prepared text. Later, they will move on to collecting information in a writing frame or entering it into a database. These activities will take considerably longer than the early activities. It is important to plan for pupils working on a project over a number of sessions.

It is important to identify whether the new learning will take place within the curriculum area or will involve the ICT. For example the Year 6 pupils in Teaching example 2.6 were using Excel to investigate a number problem. The problem was one they could have tackled with paper and pencil methods and they had also used spreadsheet formulae in short, focused tasks. In this example, therefore:

- the context was the solving of the problem;
- the learning involved the effective use of spreadsheet formulae, and the point that good use of ICT could ease the solving of repetitive number problems.

Reflective tasks

When you are next planning a teaching session involving ICT exploration within another subject area, think carefully where the new learning will be focused.

– Is the cross-curricular theme the context within which the pupils are refining and developing ICT skills?

– Is the ICT being used to support and enhance new learning in the cross-curricular area?

Read Teaching example 2.6, in the previous chapter, and try to envisage how you would have planned the session.

Practical task

Use Teaching example 2.6 as a starting point for planning an exploration session of your own.

When planning to use ICT in a teaching session it is important to consider what the benefits of using ICT are. If the pupils can explore and gain worthwhile experience in other ways, and if the use of ICT is not specifically adding something to their experience, then ICT is not necessary and should not be used.

Differentiation and inclusion

Differentiation needs to be planned and should be provided for through a range of activities and resources. Some children may require more or less support; others may require specific resources to help them access the curriculum. Children with less experience or less confidence with ICT will need additional support until their confidence increases. This could be an adapted task to suit their needs, or additional adult support (possibly a Teaching Assistant working alongside them).

Many software applications offer different ranges of activities within a broad theme. You as the teacher can select the levels within the program the children will be working with, or the controls they will have access to.

Children with identified special needs have the same entitlement as all other pupils. However, their needs may mean that the way in which they access the curriculum has to be adjusted. Pupils with physical or communication difficulties may require specially adapted hardware such as keyboards or a mouse.

Concept keyboards, which have a grid of pressure-sensitive areas, can be used as an alternative to the standard QWERTY keyboard. Concept keyboards are highly versatile and the pressure-sensitive grid can be used to send almost any information to the computer. Boards such as Intellikeys offer a range of alternative keyboard layouts. The boards are used with a paper overlay of the alphabet, can be used in conjunction with the software and the keyboard will then type individual letters when they are pressed. Since each area of the board can be programmed to give a range of inputs (individual letters, whole words, phrases or images), a pupil with special needs could work with an overlay of pictures which input phrases to help them write a story. Keyboards can be A4 or A3 in size and they offer a larger key area than the standard keyboard to help users with motor disabilities. The facility to adapt the overlays also means that overlays can be made which have high contrast lettering to help pupils with visual impairments.

Computer software is usually designed to be used by controlling an onscreen pointer with a mouse. When used with an interactive white board (IWB), this software becomes more accessible, but for pupils working with a mouse there can be considerable difficulties. To use a mouse effectively requires a high degree of manual skill and hand−eye co-ordination. Some children may find this awkward simply because of their undeveloped motor control. Children with very poor motor control may find the process very frustrating. Mouse adapters, such as SEMERC's Mouser, can help since they permit the teacher to adjust the way the mouse works, changing buttons and even turning buttons off if necessary. Some children may require specific hardware to help them, and trackballs or large mice can be used as alternatives.

Computers with touch sensitive screens offer the most direct way of interacting with the screen image. Working with these, pupils with poor motor control can use their finger or (more usually) a specific stylus to control elements of the software. This facility is particularly useful when children are developing visual skills and hand to eye co-ordination. RM Tablet PCs are the most popular in schools. Their slate design means they are portable, but still sturdy enough to survive school life. Touch screens can be used with a range of software, most notably graphic or painting applications. However, since the stylus movements imitate the actions of the mouse, it is possible to use touch-screen computers with most programs that rely on icons to control them.

Monitoring and assessing

Effective, purposeful assessment is an essential part of learning and teaching. It is important to ensure all pupils have equal access to opportunities for using ICT in their work. At the Foundation Stage, some of these opportunities may come through child initiated activities. You will need to keep records of children's preferences here, and also encourage the children to work with ICT if they have been avoiding it.

It is important that you become familiar with the level descriptors in the National Curriculum. Practise 'levelling' some pieces of work (see the practical task below). Use examples of work from the pupils in the class where you are teaching and share your ideas with the class teacher.

As much as possible, involve the children in their own assessment. Encourage them to ask questions about their work and to consider how it could be improved or developed (see further strategies in Part 5 of this book).

As children get older, and usually by Year 4, they can be involved in assessing their own work. Pupil assessment can be at a number of levels and can be supported by clear statements of learning such as shown in the pupil's ICT assessment sheet.

Practical task

Using the level descriptors in the National Curriculum for ICT, assess a range of examples of work from your next (or your previous) school. Compare them with the assessed examples work on the National Curriculum in Action website (www.ncaction.org.uk). Do you feel your assessments match the comments on the website? Share your ideas with the class teacher.

Health and safety

It is clearly important that pupils can access ICT equipment in a safe manner. As a student, it is your class teacher's responsibility to make sure that ICT equipment is used correctly and safely. However, everyone should be involved in minimising the risk. When pupils are using ICT equipment there are a number of things to consider. Firstly, there are potential risks that can be caused by continued use of ICT equipment, for example:

- **repetitive strain injury;**
- **carpal tunnel syndrome;**
- **tendonitis;**
- **computer eye strain.**

Most of these, and others, are caused (or exacerbated) by prolonged or habitual use of ICT. Therefore they are less likely to affect pupils in primary school. However, it is good practice to minimise the risks. In particular, it is helpful if you can:

- **insert breaks in long ICT sessions to reduce muscular problems or eye strain;**
- **encourage good posture;**
- **check that the lighting in the room is adequate;**
- **be aware of any health issues or special needs that may be triggered by the monitors or the data projector;**
- **supervise children at all times.**

Some issues may be outside your control; for example, workstation design should enable pupils to reach all necessary items without stretching. If this is not the case, it is unlikely that you will be able to make any changes. The only option would be to discuss your concerns (diplomatically) with the class teacher or the subject leader for ICT.

Other major safety issues revolve around the possibility of pupils accessing inappropriate material on the internet. The concept of exploration and investigation involves giving children the knowledge and skills to gather information effectively. This will include internet searching techniques. The internet is a powerful learning tool but pupils need to learn how to use it safely. They need to be protected from unacceptable material and should be given the skills to protect themselves while at school and at home. All schools should have an internet policy as part of their whole-school ICT documentation. This will outline acceptable use and the preventative measures in place to protect the pupils.

Schools (and many parents) will use web protection software to prevent accidental exposure to unacceptable material. However, children should also be made aware of ways to keep themselves safe. Websites such as www.kidsmart.org.uk offer excellent advice and information for children, parents and teachers.

Practical task

At the beginning of your next school experience ask your class teacher or the subject leader for ICT about the school's internet Acceptable Use Policy. Visit the Government Superhighway Safety website http://safety.ngfl.gov.uk/schools for further advice on this issue.

ICT strategies: exploration:

a summary of key points

——— **The National Curriculum sets out requirements for ICT regarding the knowledge and understanding which pupils should be taught.**
——— **Using ICT in differentiated teaching and learning activities, pupils develop their gross and fine motor skills, grow in self-confidence, practise and rehearse social and communication skills and develop some of the skills necessary for solving problems.**
——— **Exploring with ICT can be planned, organised, taught and assessed in a range of creative ways to enable children to find things out for themselves.**

References

NCET (1995) *Making sense of information*. Coventry: NCET.
OFSTED (2005) *Primary National Strategy: an evaluation of its impact in primary schools 2004/05*. London: HMSO.
QCA (2000) *Curriculum guidance for the foundation stage*. London: QCA.
QCA (2005) *A curriculum for the future: subjects consider the challenge*. London: QCA.

Further reading

Meadows, J. (2004) *Science and ICT in the primary school: a creative approach to big ideas.* London: David Fulton. The author provides detailed and practical guidance on how to use ICT to support creative science teaching. There is clear emphasis on learning science 'through' the technology rather than 'from' it, and a number of case studies highlight how ICT can be incorporated into cross-curricular themes.

Resources

IntelliKeys from Inclusive Technology. Further details from www.inclusive.co.uk.

Big Keys simplified computer keyboards from Keytools Ltd. Further details from www.bigkeys.co.uk.

Flexitree 2 from Flexible Software Ltd. Further details from www.flexible.co.uk/.

RM Tablet from Research Machines. Further details from www.rm.com/Primary/

Learning Ladder and **The Ultimate Human Body** from Dorling Kindersley. Further details from http://schools.dk.com/.

The Crystal Rainforest from Sherston. Further details from www.sherston.com.

4 TEXTUAL COMMUNICATION IN PRACTICE

By the end of this chapter you should:

- **be aware of how ICT can impact on children's learning;**
- **recognise the value of developing children's ICT capability;**
- **understand the relationships between ICT and written communication;**
- **be aware of effective methods of combining ICT with written communication as textual communication;**
- **recognise the value of using ICT to teach written communication skills within the literacy hour and across the curriculum;**
- **be aware of how technology is redefining literacy.**

Professional Standards for QTS
Q2.1, Q2.2, Q2.3, Q2.4, Q2.6, Q3.3

Links to the Foundation Stage Guidance and the National Curriculum

In the Foundation Stage children will find out about and identify the uses of everyday technology and use information and communication technology and programmable toys to support their learning.

At Key Stage 1 children will be involved in entering, storing and retrieving information (Ib, Ic). They will also be using text as a way of developing their ideas (2a), and sharing their ideas effectively with others (3a, 3b). Throughout this they will work with a range of information and explore a variety of ICT tools and discuss the nature of ICT in the real world (5a, 5b, 5c).

At Key Stage 2 children will be involved in preparing information, using ICT to develop it and checking it for accuracy (Ib, Ic). They will be developing and refining their ideas by organising and adapting text (2a). Children will also share and exchange information and be sensitive to the needs of the audience (3a, 3b). During this work, children will explore a variety of information sources and ICT tools as well as comparing the uses of ICT inside and outside the school (5a, 5b, 5c).

Introduction

Textual communication is the use of ICT to support the development of children's written communication skills.

ICT has fundamentally altered the way we communicate with each other. Instantaneous electronic communication is a major part of business and a large factor in all our lives. The National Curriculum places 'communication' at the heart of ICT, figuratively and literally. However, when we begin to utilise ICT as a communication tool within the school curriculum, a number of barriers appear.

Firstly, the notion of 'written communication' is all too easily seen as a function of literacy, and therefore it is most often dealt with in fractional units as part of the National Literacy Strategy.

Secondly, when ICT and 'written communication' are combined this generally equates to working with word processing software.

Finally, the requirements of helping learners become efficient users of word processing software may overtake the aims we initially had of creating effective communicators; in other words the need to develop ICT capabilities drives the learning and teaching.

Although this may seem to be a bleak and exaggerated view, in practice it is a scenario that is all too easy to move towards.

There are positives to be found, however; OFSTED has found that where ICT is used effectively, children:

- **show improved attitudes to learning through the interactive nature and visual appeal of computers and interactive white boards;**
- **are excited by the wider range of resources available to them;**
- **find the use of ICT a helpful way to share ideas and techniques;**
- **gain independence and confidence in their learning, for example pupils with special educational needs who have access to their own laptops;**
- **are motivated and consequently produce work involving greater effort and often of superior quality.**

(OFSTED, 2005, p20)

The key phrase is, of course, *where ICT is used effectively*. Only with well focused planning and carefully resourced, meaningful activities can ICT transform learning and teaching.

This chapter describes some of the strategies and activities that lead to the most effective use of ICT with written communication.

ICT and written communication

Within the school curriculum children's use of ICT and written communication falls into four sections:

1. understanding what ICT does;
2. developing ICT capabilities;

3. developing written communication skills;
4. utilising and combining ICT and written communication.

The sections are not strictly hierarchical, except that it would be unwise to begin work combining skills (section 4) without first offering the children opportunities to develop them (sections 2 and 3).

1. Understanding what ICT does

At first sight this seems to be the role of the early years practitioners to teach children how technology affects our lives. The Stepping Stones that begin children's journey of understanding in Nursery classes indicate that children should:

*   **show an interest in ICT;**
*   **know how to operate simple equipment;**
*   **complete a simple program on the computer and/or perform simple functions on ICT apparatus.**

Leading up to the child being able to:

*   **find out about and identify the uses of everyday technology and use information technology.**

(Adapted from QCA, 2000, p92)

Certainly the development starts in the Foundation Stage. It continues through discussions and work in role play, highlighting ways in which ICT helps in the real world: the children could learn about the technologies used in the home, school, shops, hospitals, newsrooms, travel agencies and even airports.

However, the National Curriculum reminds us of the need to develop children's awareness of the breadth of the impact which technology has on our lives. So discussions regarding the uses of technology in the 'real world', need to be a common feature in most classrooms throughout the key stages. Some teachers have specific planned sessions where this knowledge and understanding can be developed. Many however rely on incidents in the news or children's own interests to provide suitable opportunities. This latter, ad hoc, tactic is fraught with weaknesses, and should be particularly avoided at Key Stage 2 where children can be less willing to ask unsolicited questions and where the technicalities of the information will be more involved. A useful approach is to have a regularly changing display area which identifies some of the real-world issues surrounding the use of ICT. Inviting children to contribute to such an area is more purposeful than simply hoping that an issue will arise.

Children will also continue to gain additional understanding of the way ICT works to help (and occasionally frustrate) us throughout many daily events and occurrences, planned or otherwise. If you regularly use an interactive white board to demonstrate teaching points, for example, then children are gaining an insight into the value of ICT. It is important to remember that children are always learning and they will quickly pick up your attitude towards ICT. If you display uncertainty then children who lack confidence may feel their 'fear' is justified.

It would be wrong, however, to view ICT's contribution to written communication as simply making that communication simpler, faster and more convenient. In fact technology is influencing the very nature of written communication and literacy. The use of hyperlinks and embedded images and sounds in CD ROMs and on the internet is changing the definition of literacy. These ideas will be discussed in more detail later in this chapter and in Part 4.

2. Developing ICT capabilities

There are occasions when children need specific sessions or activities in order to develop their ICT skills. These are times when children are given opportunities and 'training' in how to effectively control the mouse (for example), or use a particular piece of software.

Simple programs such as Mouse in the House (from d2 digital by design Ltd) that involve clicking and dragging objects on the screen enable children to understand the connection between the mouse movements and screen actions. Similarly, programs that ask children to press the space bar, or use the enter key to select elements, help to develop children's early understanding of a word processor. The QCA scheme of work for ICT identifies a number of activities designed to improve young children's confidence with a word processor. Activities such as *Using a Word Bank*, *The Information Around Us* and *Writing Stories* (Units IB, IC and 2A respectively) take children from the beginnings of learning about the computer keyboard to recognising that ICT lets them correct and improve their work.

Teaching example 4.1

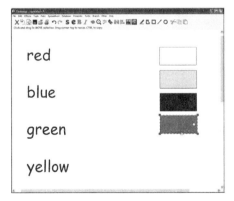

Figure 4.1. Textease for naming colours

Reception

ICT learning intention: **to control a mouse pointer to click and drag a screen element.**

Mathematical development learning intention: to recognise and read the names of the colours.

The teacher had set up an e-worksheet using Textease (from Softease Ltd). The program presented the children with a screen divided into two columns. On the left were four colour words: red, blue, green and yellow, one above the other. On the right are four blocks of colours ready to be manoeuvred into position near their name labels. The teacher asked the children about the words and the coloured blocks. They read the colours and demonstrated that they recognised the association between the words and the blocks. The teacher then helped the children to control the mouse: to move the block across to the appropriate colour-name.

It is obvious from the details in this example that the children knew enough about colours to cope with the reading and matching activity. The new learning, therefore, involved the development of their 'mouse skills'.

Reflective task

Think about the computer areas used by pupils in your placement school(s) and consider these questions.

- *Is the space where the keyboard (and mouse) are located suitable?*
- *Have books and equipment encroached into the mouse-space or otherwise become a burden to anyone working with the computer?*
- *How could you improve the environment?*

For young children the keyboard can be a bewildering place. Stickers and special, lower-case keyboards are available for the early years, but even with these there are still over 100 buttons. One solution is to eliminate the 'unnecessary' keys by placing blank stickers over them.

In the following example a teacher restricts the keyboard to simplify the task of working with CVC words (simple three letter words which fall into the pattern of consonant-vowel-consonant).

Teaching example 4.2

Year 1
ICT learning intention: to locate and use specific letter keys and the 'enter' key.

Literacy learning intention: to be confident reading and writing CVC words.

The teacher set up her classroom computer to assist a specific group of children with special needs. She blanked off the majority of the letter keys on the keyboard, and marked, in lower case, the letters: *a, b, c, d, e, g, i, n, p, t*. She also labelled the 'space bar' and 'enter' keys.

> The children were then able to produce lists of appropriate CVC words using this restricted set of keys: *bed, net, bag, cap, pig, pen, pin, pip,* etc. At the end of the session the teacher helped the children to print out their work. She asked the children to talk about the words they had found and how they could develop their work, but the main thrust of her questioning and the children's discussion was on their use of the keyboard. The final few moments of the session involved the children being invited to demonstrate how quickly they could find specific letters.

With this type of activity the ICT focus is strong, and quite specific skills are being developed, while the literacy skills are not overshadowed. Restricting to certain letter combinations has two main advantages: the children are developing their skills to identify specific letters, and their work with the keyboard is considerably simplified.

Practical task

Consider the keyboards and other equipment you have used with pupils. Are they appropriate? Would changing the letter style on the keys or labelling individual keys be helpful for the children you have worked with?

Do you have any pupils who are left-handed? Do they have any difficulties using the keyboard or mouse?

Have you worked with pupils who have special needs? Can you identify any who may benefit from specialised keyboards or alternative mouse devices?

An alternative to overloading children with the keyboard is to supplement it with another method of inputting text. There are two main ways of doing this, both of which will be discussed in greater detail.

An alternative input device, such as concept keyboards which replace or augment the existing QWERTY keyboards. Concept keyboards have large button areas with key words or images. One press of a button can type a whole word, or even a phrase.

An onscreen keyboard can also be used to supplement the traditional keyboard. Many school word processors have a word bank feature which allows for the selection of specific words with the mouse rather than typing them. Clicker 5 is a specific program which offers simple word processing elements together with comprehensive word bank features. The Clicker screen is divided horizontally. The top half is the writing area. Children can place the cursor here and write as in any word processor program. The bottom section of the screen is devoted to the word grids. These grids are word banks but individual cells of the grid can include images, words, letters, phrases, sentences or punctuation.

This section has described a range of activities which children can undertake to help them develop their ICT skills. These activities can be implemented in a computer suite where all children are working together, or through a rolling program of work on machines in the classroom. What is important is that the children have a good understanding of the ways in which ICT works to assist us and a grounding in the ways in which we can control it.

Think of these sessions or activities as 'learning **about** *ICT'.*

3. Developing written communication skills

In the Foundation Stage children gain opportunities to explore and experiment with words and texts. The link between print and meaning can be developed either within specific Communication, Language and Literacy (CLL) sessions, or as part of the children's everyday routines. At the same time young children should be exposed to electronic texts, talking books, onscreen word-lists, titles and captions on video, and through your use of electronic text onscreen or via a projector. The Curriculum Guidance for the Foundation Stage specifically mentions the role of ICT-based texts within CLL (QCA, 2000, p63).

In Key Stages 1 and 2 the National Literacy Strategy offers a framework wherein children address written communication skills in word level, sentence level and text level work.

Clearly, as in the Foundation Stage, ICT can support written communication through the use of display technologies, where the whole class reads and discusses a text during the whole-class teaching part of the session. However, display technology equipment need not be the latest expensive gadgetry.

Teaching example 4.3

Year 3

ICT learning intention: none.

Literacy learning intention: to use base joins, in a joined handwriting style.

The teacher has arranged an acetate sheet with feint handwriting guide lines on an overhead projector (OHP). One of the children is encouraged to come forward to demonstrate his handwriting by writing directly on the acetate with an OHP pen. He uses the guide lines to help him while the teacher and the rest of the children watch how he demonstrates his joins.

- This type of activity, as well as being motivational, clearly offers opportunities for direct instruction and effective assessment opportunities.

Reflective task

Is this an example of learning about, learning with, or learning through ICT?

Practical task

There were no specific learning intentions for ICT in the example above; however, children were nevertheless gaining an understanding of how simple ICT technologies can help them demonstrate work to others. Look at your planning from a recent lesson and consider whether learning about ICT may have taken place even though you had not specifically planned for it.

The nature of written communication is inescapably tied to 'literacy'. However, the theme and the flavour of the work the children meet can be adapted. The government's *Excellence and Enjoyment* document highlights this flexibility when it identifies the need to:

> support teachers and schools across the whole curriculum, building on the lessons of the Literacy and Numeracy Strategies, but moving on to offer teachers more control and flexibility. (DfES, 2003, p22)

The following example is an illustration of how a written communication focus can be enhanced by delivering elements through a history project.

Teaching example 4.4

Year 3

ICT learning intention: to use concept mapping software to organise their ideas.

History learning intention: to identify the chain of events following the start of the fire.

The children had been working on the Fire of London; the focus of their research had been the life in London at the time and events leading up to the fire. At this point their teacher decided to involve them in discussing and identifying the chain of events immediately after the start of the fire. This was partially historical fact and partially based on the children's understanding of likely events that would occur at this time. The children collected their thoughts together using 2connect, concept mapping software that enabled them to organise and adapt their ideas.

The children worked in pairs to enable them to develop and refine their ideas. When they were happy with their sequence of events they structured the account in a word processor.

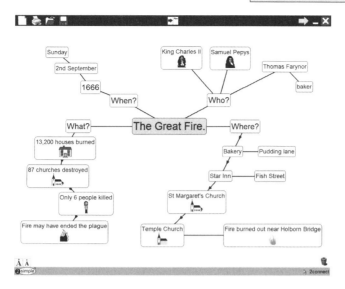

Figure 4.2. 2connect mapping

At the end of the session they shared their work with others in the class and the teacher encouraged them to discuss similarities between the accounts and then led them back to true historical events that had been recorded.

Reflective task

On your next teaching practice consider some of the literacy work you are planning; could elements of it be delivered through other subject areas?

Spelling is a discrete literacy skill. However, ICT can help with motivation and practice. Again, specific 'training' programs are available such as Wordshark and Starspell. The latter package employs a look–say–cover–write–check approach which all children will appreciate using.

The two programs mentioned above offer quite 'closed' opportunities for learning. They offer children opportunities to repeatedly practise the words in isolation, but there their usability stops. A much more versatile, and less structured, approach is to use electronic, illustrated dictionaries. These are available on CD ROM or as online resources. Talking dictionaries and observational memory games such as Memory Skills (Sherston) can support visual discrimination and phonological awareness in a more open-ended way. Many teachers also use the speech facilities built into most word processors. The clear, spoken, feedback given when a sentence is typed is very helpful to children as they begin the writing challenge.

Even with a word processor, effective teachers scaffold the children's written work by offering supports such as templates, writing frames and word banks. The following activity starts with an aerial photograph of the local area. The teacher displays the image via a data-projector on a white board. The children discuss the image and the geographical features they can see. Then, individually they are given the task of label-ling some of the features. The image was used as a 'background' in a word-processing program. The children created text boxes, selected a suitable font and manoeuvred this text label into position near the geographical feature they were labelling.

The teacher had provided an e-worksheet with ready-made labels for particular chil-dren who needed greater support with their writing.

Think about the kind of differentiated activities you offer children. What support structures do you employ with less able children? What challenges do you provide for the more confident? Differentiation by outcome, especially with written work, is rarely an effective form of differentiation.

Teaching example 4.5

Year 2

ICT learning intention: to combine text and graphics in order to convey information in a meaningful way.

Geography learning intention: to use geographical vocabulary to label familiar features, eg: hill, valley, river, road, motorway, lake, road.

The teacher used an aerial photograph of the local area as a background in a Textease word-processing program. The children were then asked to label the features they could see, using the geographical terms. They were already aware of the word processor's features and were now adding and editing text and accurately positioning the text on the screen.

The activity was designed so that the children had to think carefully about the geographical terms, to type them and then place them in appropriate locations on the image. This tight focus is important.

Another essential element of written communication is the use of 'talking books'. Talking books utilise all of the normal conventions associated with reading a book: the presentation of the pages on screen, the layout of the text and images and the ability to 'turn' the pages. However, additional learning opportunities, motivation and interest come from the interactive elements. The text is read, individual words can be clicked on and heard again and the text is usually highlighted as it is read aloud. This final element is of paramount importance, some talking books will read, and highlight, individual syllables. This offers a direct correlation between the word that is heard and the written text in a way that is not possible with a real book.

Many of the elements described in this section are clearly cross-curricular in nature. While they undoubtedly offer very real benefits to literacy sessions, they do not have to remain there. Children can work with (and actively use) OHP texts for any subject area. Multimedia electronic dictionaries can be used within science, Religious education (RE) or geography projects and electronic thesauruses can be used to improve the tone of a piece of historical writing or to amend a spiritual thought. Similarly talking books can and should feature in history, geography, RE or any other subject area. The more creative you can be with your use of ICT in written communication across the curriculum, the better.

Think of these sessions or activities as 'learning with ICT'.

4. Utilising and combining ICT and written communication

At one time there were fears that the use of technology in schools would make reading and writing less important. However, the reverse has happened. The popularity of email and 'texting' (despite the vagaries of spelling) indicates that many people are willing to swap spoken conversations for those based on reading and writing. These electronic texts are redefining literacy, and although technology has placed greater emphasis on the need to be literate, the nature of that literacy is changing. ICT has introduced new ways of reading and writing. Children need an effective range of skills to help them navigate ICT texts such as interactive, moving texts, hyperlinked texts or those which contain images or include sound and video.

Where the nature of ICT is understood by the children and they have the capability to utilise it fully, texts can be designed and presented for specific purposes. Using templates in desk top publishing (DTP) packages or the advanced features of word processing programs will enable children to create professional looking publications across a range of cross-curricular themes. This is a rich vein, of which only a few ideas can be discussed here. However, children can combine the literacy needs of focusing on language forms with a broad range of text types, such as:

- **multi-page storybooks with lettering style to suit the content, theme and audience;**
- **multi-page newsletters or pamphlets with images;**
- **using the word-count feature to produce mini-sagas of exactly 50 words;**
- **recipe leaflets with a series of pictures;**
- **a letter of complaint;**
- **a job application;**
- **a modern text message relating the details of an historic event;**
- **poster design;**
- **a scientific report with embedded charts and graphs;**
- **persuasive texts;**
- **instruction sheets for a task;**
- **a persuasive advertisement.**

Practical task

Visit the British Educational Communications and Technology Agency (Becta) advice website (www.ictadvice.org.uk) and note useful strategies for developing the use of DTP and word processing activities.

Becta's ICT Advice CD ROM (2004) offers hundreds of very detailed lesson suggestions. The following example clearly illustrates how effective use of ICT can enhance children's learning.

Teaching example 4.6

Year 3

ICT learning intention: to learn that email is a quick method of communicating with wider audiences.

Literacy learning intention: to use appropriate conventions when writing for a specific audience.

The children use email to send reviews to a website that invites submissions such as BBC's *Blue Peter*. First, let the children search through the reviews already published on the website. Which are the most and least successful – why? How long are the selected reviews? What type of information do they contain? Who do they seem to be written for?

Then ask the children to construct book reviews that reflect the type of work published on the site in terms of audience, length and content. Get them to show their work to a partner for peer review and to make any improvements necessary before getting their reviews ready for submission. Get the children to send in their reviews.
(Adapted from Becta 2004)

With this activity, ICT adds a further dimension to the writing of a review. Using email enables pupils to send reviews to a wider audience than would otherwise be possible and to see their work published on the internet. This gives them both a real audience and a purpose for their writing.

Practical tasks

Consider developing the above idea.

Email exchanges of book reviews could be arranged with another school. Alternatively, children can send drafts of their work to be edited by a member of another class.

Reading clubs could be organised so that children read specific sections of books and discuss them with their peers via email.

Find out if the school where you have your next professional placement has its own website. Talk to the subject leader for ICT to see if you can arrange to have work by your children 'published' on the site.

Examine your practice at every opportunity – if possible arrange for another teacher to observe you working with ICT and written communication. Ask them to help you to identify strengths and weaknesses, use some of the Practical Tasks in this chapter to help you focus the observation.

Continue to be vigilant when planning sessions that include ICT. Decide whether the session is going to be used to develop ICT skills or if you are using the ICT to enhance elements of the curriculum. This is not an easy decision to make but the following chapter is designed to help.

Activities like these are not 20-minute tasks. To be fully involved with the learning and make the most gains from these situations children need the opportunity and the freedom to work together for a sustained length of time. This can become an ongoing project in its own right.

Practical task

Look again at your planning. Where do you concentrate the use of ICT? Is it used solely in the introductory part of the lesson?

Consider how you can build in to your planning opportunities for children to work for an extended time, over several weeks, on individual or small group projects.

Additional features of written communication made possible through ICT include using hyperlinks. Children need to be aware of what hyperlinks look like and how to use them. CD ROM encyclopaedias or online dictionaries have set the standard of using an underline and a changing cursor icon into a 'hand' symbol. But children need to be aware of these conventions. The changing icon is occasionally the only clue that a hyperlink is present on the page, particularly where the link is part of an image.

Children can then use conventional hyperlinks in their own digital writing through word processor programs. Microsoft Word is the professional word processor most commonly used by older children, but programs designed for younger users, like Textease, also offer a hyperlink capability. Specific presentation software such as Microsoft PowerPoint also offers children the opportunity to develop the use of hyperlinks.

As in the earlier sections, almost all of the content of this section is applicable beyond the taught literacy session. The use of webquests, talking books, presentations software and email all lend themselves easily to cross-curricular work. When planning the next block of work consider how a webquest or the use of email would support learning in RE. Would the use of talking books or presentations software further enhance children's development of design technology or art work? Can you plan for these activities to be carried out over a sustained period of time?

These are just starting points and some may entail the additional use of sound, images and full multimedia features. These areas will be further explored in Part 4: Multimedia Communication.

Think of these sessions or activities as 'learning through ICT'.

Textual communication in practice:
a summary of key points

___ *Effective use of ICT can have a tremendous impact on children's learning.*
___ *Children need to gain confidence with ICT skills before they are asked to use them as part of literacy sessions.*
___ *There is a distinction between learning about, learning with, and learning through ICT.*
___ *The breadth of the ICT curriculum requires that 'communicating with text' is seen as a cross-curricular feature.*
___ *Technology is redefining the concept of 'literacy'.*

References

Abbott, C. (2001) *ICT: changing education*. London: Routledge.

Becta (2004) *ICT advice: effective use of ICT in subject teaching*. CD ROM. Coventry: Becta.

DfES (2003) *Excellence and enjoyment: A strategy for primary schools*. London: DfES

Gamble, N. and Easingwood, N. (2000) *ICT and literacy: information and communications technology, media, reading and writing*. London: Continuum.

Mumtaz, S. and Hammond, M. (2002) The word processor re-visited: observations on the use of the word processor to develop literacy at Key Stage 2. *British Journal of Educational Technology*, 3 (33): 345–7.

OFSTED (2005) *Primary National Strategy: an evaluation of its impact in primary schools 2004/05*. London: HMSO.

QCA (2000) *Curriculum guidance for the foundation stage*. London: QCA.

QCA (2005) *A curriculum for the future: subjects consider the challenge*. London: QCA

Van Daal, V. and Reitsma, P (2000) Computer-assisted learning to read and spell: results from two pilot studies. *Journal of Research in Reading*, 23 (2): 181–93.

Further reading

Gamble, N. and Easingwood, N. (2000) *ICT and literacy: information and communications technology, media, reading and writing*. London: Continuum. An examination of how technology can impact upon the teaching and learning of literacy. Details talking books, video editing, interactive multimedia and online resources.

Resources

Textease Studio from Softease Ltd. Further details from www.softease.com/.
Wordshark from White Space Ltd. Further details from www.wordshark.co.uk/.
Starspell from Inclusive Technology Ltd. Further details from www.inclusive.co.uk/.
2connect from 2simple. Further details from www.2simple.com.
Memory Skills from Sherston Publishing Group. Further details from www.sherston.com/.

5 ICT STRATEGIES: TEXTUAL COMMUNICATION

Links to the Foundation Stage Guidance and the National Curriculum

In the Foundation Stage children will find out about and identify the uses of everyday technology, and use information and communication technology and programmable toys to support their learning.

At Key Stage I children will be involved in entering, storing and retrieving information (Ib, Ic). They will also be using text as a way of developing their ideas (2a), and sharing their ideas effectively with others (3a, 3b). Throughout this they will work with a range of information and explore a variety of ICT tools and discuss the nature of ICT in the real world (5a, 5b, 5c).

At Key Stage 2 children will be involved in preparing information, using ICT to develop it and checking it for accuracy (Ib, Ic). They will be developing and refining their ideas by organising and adapting text (2a). Children will also share and exchange information and be sensitive to the needs of the audience (3a, 3b). During this work, children will explore a variety of information sources and ICT tools as well as comparing the uses of ICT inside and outside of school (5a, 5b, 5c).

Introduction

Chapter 4 illustrated examples where teachers were using ICT to help pupils develop communication skills by exchanging and sharing information. The tools and strategies discussed in this chapter will enable you to develop your understanding of the demands of the NC and the CGFS.

Communicating and presenting information is much broader than simply written text; the application of sound, animation and images impact upon the nature of the communication. This is especially important when considering the *variety of forms* element of the requirements at Key Stage 1, and where the children are required to *be sensitive to the needs of the audience* at Key Stage 2. This variety of forms, sound, images, animation, etc., will be discussed in Part 4, since they constitute aspects of multimedia.

This chapter will focus purely on tools and strategies for developing written communication skills and addressing professional issues associated with communicating in text.

Tools and strategies

Beginning to communicate with text in the Foundation Stage

In the Foundation Stage the emphasis on writing is on the actual act of writing, holding the pencil correctly, forming recognisable letters and on the fact that writing communicates meaning.

The FS children can begin to understand the ways in which ICT can help them to *share their ideas by presenting information in a variety of forms* and that it is essentially another tool for writing. The Early Learning Goals (ELGs) for writing indicate that children should:

- **attempt writing for different purposes (lists, stories, instructions) (QCA, 2000, p64);**
- **write their names, and other things such as labels and captions and begin to form simple sentences (QCA, 2000, p64).**

Here, ICT can play its part. Although children may only be writing initial letters they are still becoming familiar with the use of a keyboard and mouse – developing the key skills which will enable them to use ICT purposefully as they develop through school. You need to consider providing opportunities for children to:

- **have specific activities where they simply type in specific letters;**
- **draw a picture and label it;**
- **write their own name;**
- **write their own name using capital letters;**
- **use software which enhances specific skills (letter/word recognition, for example);**
- **simplify the keyboard (see Teaching example 4.2);**
- **provide a range of keyboards for children's needs (lower-case letter keys, concept keyboards, Big Keys);**

- use ICT in role play;
- make ICT applications available for child-initiated activities;
- work together in order to develop their speaking and listening skills and the notion of sharing ideas.

ICT also has an impact upon children's development of reading skills. The use of talking stories such as *Oxford Reading Tree Stories* and *BBC Storycraft 1* (from Sherston) allows children to see and hear the text being spoken. Segers and Verhoeven (2002) suggest that interactive talking books can have a considerable impact on pupils' oral and written language development. The multimedia aspects help to maintain enthusiasm, and the narration and illuminated text aid the promotion of word recognition, help to demonstrate the link between written text and spoken word and reinforce the left–right reading writing convention. All these factors help the pupils to recognise that writing is important, and that the information it delivers has a consistent message. The need for pupils to access written text in this way is emphasised in the Curriculum Guidance, which indicates that pupils should:

- know that information can be retrieved from books and computers (QCA, 2000, p62);
- encourage children to add to their first-hand experience of the world through books, texts and ICT (QCA, 2000, p63).

Communicating with text across Key Stages 1 and 2

The Exchanging and Sharing Information strand of the Programme of Study for Key Stages 1 and 2 details that pupils should be taught the following:

Key Stage 1
3a: how to share their ideas by presenting information in a variety of forms;
3b: to present their completed work effectively.

Key Stage 2
3a: how to share and exchange information in a variety of forms including email;
3b: to be sensitive to the needs of the audience and think carefully about the content and quality when communicating information.

From the requirements of the National Curriculum and details within the QCA scheme of work it is possible to establish progression in terms of expectations and skills development for both key stages.

KEY STAGE 1
Although, at first glance, most of the skills listed here seem to be literacy based, they offer many opportunities for cross-curricular work. Much of the knowledge, understanding and skill can (and should) be developed outside the Literacy Strategy. Teaching example 4.5, in the previous chapter, outlined an activity where pupils were involved in labelling an aerial photograph. Some of the skills were clearly literacy ones, but the context and learning intentions were related to geography and ICT.

Table 5.1. Key Stage I skills

Skills	Knowledge and understanding of the controls	Examples
using the mouse to select and move words	pointer, click, select, drag	see Teaching example 4.1
using the mouse to assemble sentences	pointer, click, select, drag	incomplete sentences are presented on screen and the pupils have to click and drag text in order to complete a sentence
entering text into a word processor with a word bank or concept keyboard	delete, word bank	using a word bank or concept keyboard to spell words or write a simple account of an event
using the keyboard to enter words into a word processor	keyboard, enter, spacebar, delete/backspace	see Teaching example 4.2
using a word processor to produce sentences that communicate meaning	keyboard, enter, spacebar, delete/backspace shift key, full stop	use the keyboard to write a simple story or an account of a science investigation using appropriate punctuation
refining sentences by adding words or making corrections	keyboard, enter, spacebar, delete/backspace shift key, full stop, cursor, mouse, highlight, insert	adapt or amend prepared text using word processor tools
exploring and using a range of fonts, text colours, sizes and decorations	font, text, size, style, bold, underline, italic, cursor, mouse, highlight	adapt a prepared piece of text (such as a poem) by using a range of text decorations
beginning to use some of the advanced features of a word processor to organise and layout text	insert, textbox, resize, cursor, arrow keys	see Teaching example 4.5

Depending on the children's previous experience and capabilities, some skills may already have been developed in the Foundation Stage.

Reflective task

On your next school placement look carefully at the school's long-term planning or the scheme of work that they use. Consider the following points.

- *What cross curricular opportunities are there?*
- *How does it build on the knowledge and skills taught in the Foundation Stage?*
- *How is skills progression ensured through the plan/scheme?*

A key feature of the use of ICT is its provisionality – the freedom it gives users to make changes. Pupils are making effective use of this 'provisionality' while developing most of the above skills. They can change text size, font style or colour or emphasise words; they can reorder individual words, or move sentences and sections of text. All these changes can be made instantly, and undone without any trace being left. These are powerful features, which are simply not possible with paper and pencil techniques. A reluctant or hesitant writer can be encouraged to produce higher qual-ity work, and will, usually, be more enthusiastic about their work when it involves a word processor (this aspect of ICT work is dealt with in greater detail in Part 5).

KEY STAGE 2
Building on the work carried out at Key Stage I (and considering the NC require-ments for Key Stage 2, as well as elements from the QCA scheme of work for ICT), further stages of progression can be identified. The following table suggests some of these.

Table 5.2. Key Stage 2 skills

Skills	Knowledge and understanding of the controls	Examples
combining graphics with text	cut, copy, paste, resize, scale, insert	create a class magazine using images and captions (QCA Scheme, unit 3A)
using appropriate fonts to meet the needs of the audience	font, text, size, style, bold, underline, italic, cursor, mouse, highlight, wordart, centre, left justify, right justify	create a poster advertisement using a range of text decorations
using spell-check and find-and-replace features to help edit work	cursor, highlight, insert, spellcheck, find, replace	edit and amend a range of texts
choosing appropriate word processing features and tools to increase efficiency	copy, cut, paste, find and replace, spellcheck – use of shortcuts	collect information from a variety of sources and combine it in a single booklet
using more advanced word processing features (or desktop publishing applications) to match the needs of the audience	copy, cut, paste, shortcuts, find and replace, split-view, spellcheck, thesaurus, bullet points – use of shortcuts	convert a sophisticated internet article so that it is readable and understandable by a younger audience
using email to communicate effectively	address, subject, send, receive, attach	see Teaching example 4.6
Depending on the children's previous experience and capabilities, some skills may already have been developed in Key Stage 1.		

Naturally, many of the skills listed depend on the pupils' confidence and their access to resources. It may be that Key Stage I pupils will be utilising skills identified with Key

Stage 2, or vice versa. Technology has developed considerably since the development of the National Curriculum, and some elements are now technically easier to achieve than they were. For example, the use of email applications is clearly identified as part of the Key Stage 2 programme of study, but greater access to these facilities has made it feasible that children in Key Stage 1 (or even the Foundation Stage) may experience working with email.

Many of the skills developed with word-processing applications can be further refined with desktop publishing (DTP) software, like PagePlus or Textease Studio, which offer pupils more sophisticated tools for creating brochures, newsletters, greetings cards, posters or leaflets. Greater sophistication of tools, however, does not automatically mean greater level of difficulty. Many of the tools within most DTP applications have automatic features which make them, on the whole, straightforward to use. The majority of applications also feature ready-made examples in a 'wizard' guide that users can adapt. This is a useful starting point, and means that certain elements, like picture layout, can be set. Pupils working with this kind of application can, therefore, access it on a number of levels. Those with less confidence and weaker skills can use a prepared template as a starting point; others may be able to generate a completely new layout for themselves.

In a similar way to DTP, the skills pupils develop with word processing can be further refined with multimedia authoring applications. Multimedia is the appropriate combination of images, sound, video and text. Presentation software, such as PowerPoint, offers a good starting point for this type of work. When working with multimedia, pupils are fully extending their communication skills; the features within the applications meaning that the pupils need to be fully aware of the needs of their audience. All these skills are clearly underpinned by the children's good communication/literacy skills. Many of these activities will be discussed in Part 4: Multimedia Communication.

Practical task

Becta (2003) have outlined a number of aspects where technology can enhance teaching and learning (see below). If you have taught sessions using ICT, consider your previous planning in light of the following points. How far have you been able to offer pupils opportunities to engage in these activities?

It is suggested that the technology can enable pupils to:

- **manipulate and transform their own and others' writing using a word processor and other publishing packages**
- **develop an understanding of language and their own critical literacy skills**
- **engage with key characteristics and features of texts**
- **discuss the merits and limitations of particular text types**
- **compare a range of ways that information is presented**
- **talk, read and write for a range of purposes and communicate with a wider group of people, thereby encouraging different types of interaction and promoting collaborative learning**

(Adapted from Becta, 2003, p1)

Professional issues

Many of the Teaching examples have illustrated that the use of a word processor changes the act of writing; it becomes much more dynamic. The ease with which changes can be made and the look of the finished work are both major contributors to children's motivation in writing. There are clear gains in the levels of achievement by pupils who use word processing with teacher guidance; they significantly improve their writing, as do those pupils who write for a real audience using the internet or email (Becta, 2003).

However, although word processing is the most commonly used feature of ICT in schools, it can be argued that its potential is not always fully exploited (Mumtaz and Hammond, 2002). Many teachers reported in the literature are only using word processing as a presentation tool for pupils, converting previously hand written notes into 'best' for display.

This is not the most effective use of ICT. It is essential, therefore, to plan and organise specific, purposeful and productive ICT work. Only with concise and effective planning in place will you and the pupils have a good understanding of the development that will be carried out during a particular teaching session.

Planning and organisation

When planning to use ICT as part of written communication, it is important that you as the teacher make decisions about why and how it will be used. These decisions should be based on whether the use of ICT supports good practice.

- **Does the use of ICT allow you to achieve something that would not have been possible without it? For example, you can use a set of flash-cards to help pupils develop their sight vocabulary. The same flash-cards set into a presentation can be displayed larger (on a white board), can be set to automatically change after a number of seconds, can easily be controlled by you or the pupils, and the whole set of cards can be duplicated, changed or extended almost instantaneously.**
- **Does the use of ICT allow the pupils to achieve something more effectively and efficiently than would be possible without it? For example, pupils can rearrange sections of handwritten text on paper by cutting the paper into strips and rearranging it. The same activity done with 'copy and paste' on a word processor is far more efficient.**

If the use of ICT does not enable either of the above (or both) then it should not be used.

Practical task

Think back to your last school experience. How often did you use ICT (such as an IWB) just because it was there, without considering whether it improved or enhanced the learning in the session?

It is important that you think carefully about the learning outcomes and the skills the children will be using and developing; is there a clear link between the two? How can the link be strengthened? Also, are there any hindrances within the set-up, design or organisation of the lesson?

Many teachers feel that despite the immense benefits of using an IWB, the fact that it can be uncomfortable and awkward to write on is a major drawback for some lessons. The surface is slick and smooth; the pen is not the best design for children to hold; in some older models the pen is designed around the batteries it must hold; in others there is considerable nib movement when the pen makes contact with the board. The digital ink can appear a little to one side of the actual nib's contact with the board, and (depending upon the effectiveness of the installation) the pupil's shadow can temporarily block out elements of the screen. This can easily become an uncomfortable and unnecessarily cumbersome method of writing for young children.

If your focus is handwriting formation then using a 'light' pen on an IWB is not necessarily the best use of ICT. The example given earlier of writing on an acetate for an OHP had more benefits: the writing surface is horizontal, which is more natural, and the text the children were expected to produce, using fine OHP pens, was a more standard size. Duplicating this on a wall mounted IWB would add difficulties for the children, effectively making the learning outcomes more distant and difficult than if the children were to simply use 'traditional' methods such as paper and pen. In fact a chalk stick on sugar paper has tremendous advantages over the IWB. The texture of the contact between the chalk and the paper gives good feedback which adds to, rather than detracts from, the learning processes.

If the ICT is not directly adding something of use to the session, do not us it. Do not plan to use it simply because it is there. The awkwardness of working on a vertical IWB has led some schools to experiment with placing the board at an angle to the wall, so the board leans back more like a painting easel. This makes working on the board easier. Hand movements are less awkward and the projector line is also improved so that the child's shadow does not get in the way of the beam and, because the board is no longer vertical, children sitting in front of it no longer see glare bouncing from sections of it.

Similarly, when thinking about subject work it is important to ask if the use of ICT will make the teaching of those learning outcomes, and pupils' learning, more effective.

Practical task

When planning for your next school placement, consider the following points.

- **In what ways will available ICT resources be most useful during the different organisational phases of a lesson?**
- **When will the use of ICT be appropriate or inappropriate?**
- **Are the ICT resources adequate for the intended purpose?**

There is a broader nature to ICT; Teaching example 4.3 illustrated a session where a teacher used an overhead projector to help demonstrate letter joins. This is effective use of an often overlooked piece of equipment. ICT goes far beyond the computer. Some schools are utilising their pupils' strong desire to send text messages and have incorporated the use of texting into a number of their lessons. Others are trialling the use of podcasts, involving the pupils in writing, recording and publishing online 'radio' broadcasts on the school website. Some of these are innovative and very useful developments, riding on the back of rapidly developing technologies. The schools operating these are in the minority, and it is uncertain at this stage exactly what real long-term learning benefits such innovative practice will bring. However, it is perfectly possible for you to use ICT in a broader sense.

Practical task

Consider wider applications for ICT. For example, how could you purposefully utilise the school photocopier within part of a teaching session?

- *What learning intentions could successfully be covered by the children using the machine?*
- *What cross-curricular learning and teaching could be drawn from such an exercise?*

ICT in literacy lessons is most often used as part of the introductory session, as shared text. This is effective for the teacher since the content can be rapidly changed. Also, with the use of a data projector and large font, it is far more useful than a traditional 'big book'. However, holding the full attention of the class can be problematic. The professional development materials from the Primary National Strategy offer a number of strategies for involving all children in whole-class teaching. Some of these can be adapted for use with ICT and should be planned for.

Strategies for planning to involve all children in whole-class teaching

- Children demonstrating to the whole class:
  - adding labels to a diagram on an interactive whiteboard.

- Pausing and asking children to predict what comes next:
  - this clearly works while turning the pages of a big book, and the activity can also be modelled when moving from one screen of text to another. Presentation software (or flipchart software) will allow pausing – keep the amount of text on each page to a minimum.

- Children creating Mind-maps, either using whiteboards or with an adult as scribe:
  - using 2connect, for example, you can model the collaborative process before the children work in groups – links with Teaching example 4.4.

- Children undertaking short practice tasks, such as writing or drawing on individual whiteboards or using number fans:
  - the above strategy can be adapted to the use of digital technology whereby in a computer suite, or with a set of laptops, the children use their screens as mini

white boards; children could also be working collaboratively to add temporary notes.

(Adapted from DfES, 2004)

Practical task

When in your next school, ask to see a copy of the professional development materials (Primary National Strategy) and note down any further teaching strategies that would be useful to you when planning to teach your next class.

Differentiation and inclusion

Planning will need to take account of the differing needs of the children, their previous experiences, levels of confidence and their capability. Clearly, the information you will need for this will come from your assessment, or from a previous teacher's assessment, of the children. You will need to provide specific activities for some pupils in order for them to make effective progress. For pupils with special needs, further specific support may be needed; this could be in the form of hardware (equipment, keyboards, etc) or software. (See the Differentiation and Inclusion section in Chapter 3, for further support.)

ICT can enable pupils with visual impairment to access the curriculum by providing alternative methods of reading and recording their work. Here are a number of starting points to be considered.

- **Word processors enable the background colour and the colour, size and type of font to be changed to suit individual pupils' needs.**
- **Screen glare may need to be reduced by the use of filters.**
- **If a pupil finds accessing the keyboard problematic, coloured or high-contrast labels can be fixed over the keys. Alternatively, the use of a concept keyboard or Big Keys may be of assistance.**
- **The option to adjust the print size makes it possible to print written work in a range of type sizes to suit the needs of individual pupils.**
- **Word processors with text-to-speech features can be used to read out screen text.**

Monitoring and assessing

As QCA have indicated:

> many teachers still find the assessment of ICT capability a challenge, and the Office for Standards in Education (OFSTED) identifies the use of assessment in planning for progression as an area of weakness in too many schools. (QCA, 2005, p4)

It is therefore important to consider both how you will assess pupils' capabilities and how you will use that assessment information in your future planning.

Often it is easier to record the activity the pupil has undertaken than to assess their ICT capability. Some suggestions for developing the assessment of pupils' ICT capability with written communication are suggested here.

- **Observe specific pupils while they are working on their activities, make notes of the capabilities they exhibit and the areas where they need further support.**

- **Ask a Teaching Assistant to work closely with specific children, keeping a record of the amount of support they have needed.**

- **Question pupils about the activity they have completed and encourage them to demonstrate some of the processes they went through.**

- **Encourage pupils to record their own progress by using self-assessment sheets which they complete themselves. In the Foundation Stage these can be simplified so that icons or images represent some of the skills. A drawing of a keyboard can have keys coloured in to denote appropriate levels of skill. For example, the children colour the backspace key, arrow keys or space bar to indicate their proficiency. Older pupils can keep a more elaborate 'I can use …' record. This could even be a word-processed document.**

- **Engage the children in setting their own targets for progress, reflecting on their own work and identifying what they need to know (or learn) next.**

- **Encourage pupils to save early drafts of their work (or print them out) so that the process they went through to arrive at their final work is easier to see.**

- **Plan for short, focused tasks (or challenges) that engage the pupils in completing an activity in a given time.**

- **Build in time at the end of a session, or the block of work, for the pupils to discuss what they have done; particularly to identify what they feel they have learnt and the skills they now feel confident with.**

Whenever children are working with ICT, the capabilities they are developing can be divided into two groups:

a) The development of technical skills and competencies. These are demonstrated, for example, by the pupils' abilities to:

- use the hardware (mouse, keyboard, CD ROMs);
- use a range of software applications.

b) The development of the pupils' deeper knowledge and understanding of ICT functions. These are demonstrated, for example, by the pupils being able to:

- make presumptions about the use and function of tools and icons based on previous knowledge;
- decide which software application or tool is appropriate for the task.

Practical task

Consider the assessment tools you have used in the past. Have you mainly assessed pupils' capabilities from group a) above, or group b)?

What could you do to enhance your assessment practice so that you are assessing capabilities from both groups?

Health and safety

Potential health and safety issues, together with your ideas for minimising them, must be included in your planning. Many of the major issues which directly affect health and safety are discussed in other chapters. However, one issue directly related to written communication is cyberbullying. This is an unpleasant side-effect of the advances in communication that technology has brought about. Cyberbullying is partially the result of the relative anonymity which emails or text messages seem to offer. Pupils may receive emails or text messages which have been sent with the intention of embarrassing, intimidating or bullying them.

Understanding the problem, and having a number of strategies available for dealing with it, can help reduce the risks. Firstly, pupils should be advised not to reveal their mobile phone number, and to ask those friends who do have their number not to pass it on.

If they receive an upsetting message, either SMS text or email, children should take the following action.

- **Seek help from a teacher, parent or carer.**
- **Not respond to the messages. If possible they should save it in case it is needed later as evidence, or keep a note of the content of the message, the date, the time and the caller ID (for text messages).**
- **Report the issue to their mobile phone company. In most circumstances the company will be able to investigate the complaint and suggest ways of resolving the situation. Ultimately, it may also be necessary to involve the police.**

If an unpleasant email is sent from a personal email account, the abuse should certainly be reported to the sender's email service provider. Like mobile phone companies, internet service providers are legally obliged to investigate these incidents. Again, they will be able to offer support and will suggest ways of resolving the situation. Most email applications also provide security features to block email from specific senders.

Even with all these precautions in place, an unwanted message can be upsetting and unsettling. In some cases it may be easier for the person affected to change their mobile phone number, or email address, and exercise great care over sharing these new details.

ICT strategies: textual communication:
a summary of key points

_____ *The National Curriculum sets out requirements for ICT regarding the knowledge and understanding which pupils should be taught.*

_____ *The most effective way to combine the use of ICT with written communication is to ensure that the learning intentions for both communication (English teaching, CLL or literacy) and ICT are clearly identified in your planning.*

_____ *Written communication with ICT should be seen as cross-curricular and be introduced and developed in the primary classroom.*

_____ *ICT should only be used if it directly enhances learning and/or teaching. It should not be used purely to enhance the 'look' of written material.*

_____ *Effective use of specific ICT resources (applications and software) can enable pupils with special needs to access the curriculum.*

_____ *There is an identifiable progression of ICT skills in written communication.*

_____ *It is important to assess pupils' developing capabilities with ICT, not just the activities they have undertaken. It is equally important to make purposeful use of these assessments when planning subsequent teaching sessions.*

References

Becta (2003) *What the research says about using ICT in English.* Coventry: Becta.

DfES (2004) *Excellence and enjoyment: learning and teaching in the primary years. Professional development materials.* London: DfES Publications.

Mumtaz, S. and Hammond, M. (2002) The word processor revisited: observa-tions on the use of the word processor to develop literacy at Key Stage 2. *British Journal of Educational Technology*, 3 (33): 345–7.

QCA (2000) *Curriculum guidance for the foundation stage.* London: QCA.

QCA (2005) *2004/5 annual report on curriculum and assessment.* London: QCA.

Segers E. and Verhoeven L. (2002) Multimedia support of early literacy learning. *Computers and Education*, 39: 207–21.

Further reading

Bennett, R. (2006) *Using ICT in primary English teaching (teaching handbooks).* Exeter: Learning Matters. An invaluable resource for teachers wanting to develop their knowledge of the ways in which ICT can support English teaching. The book draws upon research and inspection evidence, and examines ways in which ICT can be used to enhance learning and teaching. It offers a range of classroom activities and discusses organisational and management ideas, and has a very useful section on software and websites.

Resources

Oxford Reading Tree Talking Stories and **BBC Storycraft 1** from Sherston. Further details from www.sherston.com.

PagePlus from Serif. Further details from www.serif.com.

Big Keys simplified computer keyboards from Keytools Ltd. Further details from www.bigkeys.co.uk.

PART 4: MULTIMEDIA COMMUNICATION

6 MULTIMEDIA COMMUNICATION IN PRACTICE

By the end of this chapter you should:

- *have an understanding of the broad nature of 'multimedia';*
- *be aware of the range of ways in which ICT can support subject learning;*
- *recognise the motivational advantages of using ICT;*
- *be aware of the links between multimedia applications and different learning styles;*
- *be aware of the different stages of complexity within multimedia applications.*

Professional Standards for QTS
Q2.1, Q2.2, Q2.4, Q2.6, Q3.3

Links to the Foundation Stage Guidance and the National Curriculum

In the Foundation Stage children will use information communication technology to support their learning.

At Key Stage 1 children will gather information from a variety of sources and share their ideas by presenting information in a variety of forms (1a, 3a). Children will also work with a range of information to investigate the different ways it can be presented, explore a variety of ICT tools and talk about the uses of ICT outside and inside school (5a, 5b, 5c).

At Key Stage 2 children will prepare information for development using ICT, share and exchange information in a variety of forms and think carefully about the content when communicating information (1b, 3a, 3b). Throughout their work children should work with others to explore a variety of information sources, and be involved in investigating and comparing the uses of ICT inside and outside school (5b, 5c).

Introduction

Multimedia is the integration of a variety of forms of media within one program. Many websites incorporate the richness of multimedia when they combine textual elements with clip art, digital photographs, sound, animations and video. Although it sounds complex the use of multimedia approaches is quite common in most schools; indeed, most classrooms have elements of multimedia ongoing for most of the day. These forms of multimedia may come from CD ROM programmes such as talking books or animated mathematical activities. Multimedia is also used within presentation software. Microsoft PowerPoint, for example, is a very popular way of combining text, images, animation and sound. The ease with which multimedia applications can be used is continuously developing and their popularity is increasing. Consequently schools are rapidly adopting new practices. For example, some schools have begun to use podcasts as elements within their teaching sessions. Children write, edit and then record a magazine-style radio show. These are then loaded as podcasts onto the school's website where parents and other children can access them. Other schools are also working with digital video, again utilising quite new technology as part of their classroom work. While these very imaginative uses of multimedia are interesting (they will be dealt with in more detail in the next chapter), they are still fairly rare. Therefore, the main body of this chapter will deal with what are currently more widely used multimedia applications.

Multimedia applications are even more appealing when combined with an interactive white board (IWB). If you have used, or observed a teacher using, an IWB with a group of children you will be aware of how motivating the technology can be. The rise in popularity of multimedia is certainly due to the advances and greater accessibility of technology, but educational theory also seems to offer some support for using it. Fleming (2001) indicates that although some children may prefer to learn visually, others could focus on learning through auditory senses and others kinaesthetically. In their planning and delivery of sessions, teachers need to take account of the possibility that some children may find it difficult to learn in certain ways. While the notion of learning styles should not be used as a form of labelling, it is clearly effective if teachers can design learning opportunities that enable children to meet (and use) a variety of learning styles. Clearly, multimedia applications which combine text, sound and animation offer one possible way of supporting this.

Relatively simple software applications like PowerPoint also provide opportunities for children to design and produce their own multimedia work for others to share. Most multimedia packages are based on the ability to dynamically link together a series of computer screens or slides with hyperlinks or buttons.

When working with multimedia in the classroom there are essentially four ways in which it can be used.

1. Multimedia used by the teacher.
2. Multimedia used by the teacher and children together.
3. Children using multimedia applications prescribed by the teacher.
4. Children developing their own multimedia applications.

The remainder of this chapter will consider the uses of multimedia in these four ways.

I. Multimedia used by the teacher

The initial demonstration stage keeps the technology in the teacher's hands, although often children are encouraged to participate. The role of the technology is generally to help the teacher to demonstrate or clarify concepts.

Multimedia as a demonstration tool, enhanced by the use of IWBs, possibly has most potential during the initial stages of a taught session. This is particularly evident at Key Stages 1 and 2. Within numeracy or literacy sessions, for example, it is possible to make very effective use of multimedia applications during the introductory teaching element.

In numeracy, IWBs can be used to display a range of multimedia applications, for example interactive 100 squares with the facility to instantly highlight individual digits, whole columns or rows of numbers. This type of resource can help when explaining number patterns, or clarify demonstrations of a new computational strategy. Again (as in Teaching example 6.1 below), as well as easing the demonstration a multimedia application simplifies the set up and resetting process for the teacher.

Multimedia interactive applications can, similarly, support literacy teaching. Interactive texts can be shared with the children, the multimedia features of which may mean that:

- **elements of the text can be animated or instantly coloured (when highlighting phonemes, syllables or suffixes, for example);**
- **sections of text can be linked to images (for definitions, or to support work on parts of speech, for example);**
- **textual elements can be reordered (for alphabetical or dictionary work, for example).**

Clearly, multimedia applications have great potential for introducing and demonstrating concepts and ideas in all curriculum areas.

Practical task

When you are next using an IWB as part of whole-class teaching consider the following points.
- *Are you fully confident with the way the software works?*
- *How can you ensure that the children are engaged with the learning?*

If children lack confidence with ICT then multimedia can feel like a safe way of utilising ICT within a classroom. However, remember that if children are generally acting as an audience for a presentation they are not necessarily fully engaged with the learning process.

2. Multimedia used by the teacher and children together

Most teaching sessions utilising multimedia go further than the simple exposition, or demonstration, model discussed earlier. In most sessions the teacher demonstration will lead into a shared exploration, with the children now actively involved in using the multimedia resources. However, it is important to note that the teacher will still need to spend some time modelling the process before young children are introduced to working with these applications. Once children are involved, the teacher should continue to support and scaffold the learning until the children have developed the confidence to work independently.

The following example clearly begins with the teacher in exposition mode, but the invitation to the children to the board was planned and was part of the learning intention. As the children are interacting with the ICT, their peers and the teacher, this enhances their learning through social interaction.

Teaching example 6.1

Nursery

ICT learning intention: to drag objects using an IWB.

Mathematical development learning intention: to name and sort simple 2D shapes: square, triangle, and circle.

Throughout the week the children had explored shape in the environment; they had discussed and worked with 2D shapes. For this session the teacher had prepared a shape matching program on the computer. The teacher worked with a small group of children and had planned to use the data projector along with an IWB to engage the children in working with shapes. The teacher used a simple program to display several two-dimensional shapes on the IWB. The program allowed for the manipulation of the shapes; they could be easily manoeuvred around the board by touching them. The teacher invited the children to talk about the shapes they could see and then asked each child in turn to move the shapes around the board to form a pattern, or a picture. While each child created their patterns she encouraged the other children to talk about the shapes, to guess the kind of pattern that was being created and to talk about how the shapes were being moved.

When each child had finished she asked them to talk about the pattern and to describe it. Finally, the teacher encouraged each child to sort the shapes that had been used. She asked the children which shapes are square and which are triangles, and then encouraged the children to separate the shapes … can they slide all the squares to one side of the board and the triangles to the other?

Reflective task

Think about the last time you used or observed a teacher using an IWB in a classroom situation.

Were the children involved and engaged? All of them?

If not, make a list of possible strategies you could employ in the future to maintain their involvement.

There are some specific advantages to using this type of program in this way. The motivational effects of using an IWB are considerable. Although the same results could be obtained by children using large magnetic shapes (or even card shapes with non-permanent attachments) the same movement and sorting capability would have been possible. However, for the teacher, resetting the shapes would have been more time consuming; and, for the children, the fascination that projected images offer, the vibrancy of the colour and the potential to bring in other media such as sound effects and animation would be missing. The children appeared to be fully involved in this activity and the organisation for the teacher was quick and easy.

There is, however, a limitation that needs to be considered: using coloured images of shapes, however vibrant and interactive, is not a replacement for hands-on experience. The children can count the corners of the shapes and touch the screen where the shapes are projected, but they cannot have any direct contact with the shapes themselves. When they move a projected image around on an IWB there is no tactile feedback, they are only really touching part of the screen, not a shape. Similarly, this activity offers no opportunities to feel and explore the edges or the corners of the shapes. In this sense, the versatility of using real plastic shapes would be much greater, since children can handle them and fully explore all of their features.

Reflective task

Think how the lack of hands-on experience can be overcome in activities like this. Are there better approaches?

How could you adapt this activity for children with special needs? Think about those with mobility problems or sight impairment.

Practical task

When you are next using an IWB as part of classroom teaching consider the following points.

- *Is the space in front of the board clear? Do children have access?*
- *Does the software have tools or buttons at the bottom of the screen so that children can easily use them?*
- *Do you need to provide a small staged area so young children can access all of the board?*

The following example details a teacher's use of a simple science program that enables the children to explore the creation of electrical circuits. As in the previous example, the use of multimedia offers the advantages of efficient set-up and repeated use. However, this is at the cost of first-hand experience. The children in this example had spent several sessions working with 'real' equipment and the teacher intended the use of the software here to be part of the children's assessment.

Teaching example 6.2

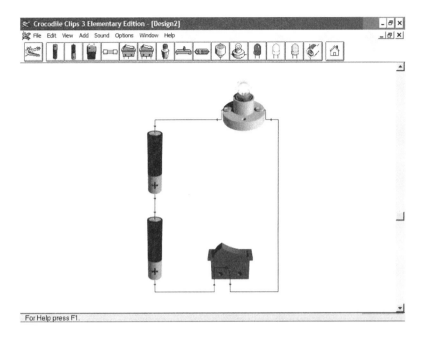

Figure 6.1. Crocodile clips electric circuit modelling program

Year 3

ICT learning intention: to use ICT to model the construction of a simple circuit using images and text.

Science learning intention: to design and label circuit diagrams using a range of lights, batteries, switches, buzzers and connectors.

Working on an individual computer in the main classroom, the teacher demonstrated the use of crocodile clips in an electric circuit modelling program. The children watched and suggested simple circuits that could be made, and then the teacher asked each child to take turns to create a circuit. The teacher had prepared a worksheet with a 'shopping list' of components and a simple task such as 'light two bulbs so that they are both controlled by one switch'.

The children then had ten minutes to complete their circuit diagram, add labels for the components and print out the work.

Practical task

Identify a session in your future teaching where it would be appropriate to use a multimedia application. Make a note of the key learning intentions you would hope to achieve.

3. Children using multimedia applications prescribed by the teacher

Once the children have had an opportunity to experience a number of multimedia applications they should have sufficient confidence to work independently. The next Teaching example illustrates how an online multimedia resource, Bobinogs (from BBC Wales), was used by individual pupils to help reinforce their understanding of some of the features of living things.

Teaching example 6.3

Figure 6.2. Bobinogs website

Nursery

ICT learning intention: to use a mouse to select screen elements.

Knowledge and understanding of the world learning intention: to find out about, and identify, some features of living things.

The children had spent some time finding out about pets and how to look after them. They had looked at pictures and models of different animals and discussed their similarities and differences. Together with the teacher they had transformed the role play area into a veterinary surgery. The teacher had also set the computer so that the children could access the BBC's Bobinogs website. The children were encouraged to work on the online activity with a nursery assistant. The activity required them to watch a short animation and then choose appropriate food, drinks and other items for a dog. The nursery assistant encouraged the children to use their knowledge of the needs of pets in order to complete the activity, and also assessed their understanding. The activity required the children to use effective mouse control to work through the task.

This type of online activity uses animation and sound to very good effect. The children are clearly consolidating their learning about some of the features and needs of animals, as well as developing their listening skills and physical development.

The next Teaching example illustrates how multimedia applications can advance children's understanding of number work. The children had spent time working on a range of practical number tasks, the teacher then encouraged the children to use a mathematical multimedia application to support their development.

Teaching example 6.4

Figure 6.3. Fizzy's First Numbers
(Reproduced by kind permission of the Sherston Publishing Group)

Reception
ICT learning intention: **to use a mouse to accurately select screen elements and buttons.**

Mathematical development learning intention: **to recognise numerals 1–9.**

As part of their work on number recognition, the children used a mathematical CD, Fizzy's First Numbers (hidden numbers activity). In this activity the numerals are partially hidden behind objects in a picture. The children have to use their knowledge of numeral shapes to identify the number. The activity requires that the children use effective hand-eye coordination and mouse control to complete the task.

The use of sound and animation in the application helps children to focus directly on the activity; the use of sound assists children to link numeral to number name with particular emphasis on the correct pronunciation of the number names. In addition an animated sequence enables the children to see and follow the written formation of the numeral.

This activity used published software which the children worked with; however, it is also possible to create a range of multimedia activities using word-processing packages such as Textease. Here, you can create pages with pictures or images which the children need to manipulate. Textease also offers straightforward ways of combining animated features and sound.

In the following example the teacher worked with a literacy theme with the focus being reading. The teacher was working with children who had special educational needs and were having difficulty with the left to right reading conventions. This lesson was also intended to reinforce one to one word correspondence; identifying that the word highlighted was in fact the word spoken.

Teaching example 6.5

Year 1

ICT learning intention: to use the conventions of a talking book.

Literacy learning intention: to identify the left–right convention of the written word.

Initially the teacher demonstrated the functions of a talking book. The teacher showed them the format of the book, the way the pages turn, the effects of clicking on images and allowed them to listen to the text being read. The children were encouraged to follow the written words which were highlighted as they listened to the story.

The children were then given the opportunity to read and explore the book in pairs.

There are clear ICT gains here, the children are involved in learning and practising specific ICT skills. The teacher also encouraged them to compare these skills to the more traditional reading skills. The ICT therefore supported the left–right reading conventions and the locations and uses of pictures. Again, the sound facility, the narration of the text, enhanced the link between spoken and written word. The animation promoted motivation and encouraged children to explore the rich environment of the book as well as focus on the text.

The children were working in pairs when they read the book themselves. The teacher explained that they should change places after a few pages so that each child could have an opportunity to use the mouse to control the turning of the pages, narration effects and the image animation effects.

Reflective task

What other strategies have you seen or used to achieve full engagement, attention and focus on learning when children are paired at the computer?

Teaching example 6.6

Figure 6.4. Mouseimage

Reception

ICT learning intention: to use a mouse to accurately select screen elements and buttons.

Creative development – musical learning intention: to create a simple sound sequence.

The teacher chose this CD ROM activity to be part of the child initiated activities available during the day in the Reception class. There had been an ongoing theme of 'music' for the week within the class and now the children had an opportunity to explore the Picture Songs activity. The children could select from a range of instrument icons, each icon represented a different musical melody. By combining several the children could produce a simple tune.

Each child spent a few minutes experimenting with the different sounds the instruments made and then produced a short melody.

At the end of the session the teacher encouraged the children to talk about their tune and they were able to share some by displaying them on a white board and playing them.

The teacher selected this activity to support the same ICT learning intention as Teaching example 6.3, however the curriculum area is quite different. It was also useful here that, although the children took part in the activity on an individual level, the teacher was able to give them an opportunity to demonstrate their work to the whole class at the end of the session.

Practical task

When you are next using a multimedia resource as part of classroom teaching consider the following points.

- *How do you organise the classroom to enable the children to have equal access?*
- *At what point do you as the teacher intervene in the children's learning?*

4. Children developing their own multimedia applications

When children begin to create multimedia applications there are clear demands on their skills and confidence with ICT, so they need to have had a great deal of experience of using multimedia applications beforehand. Children need to be confident with:

- **using a word processor to manipulate text;**
- **using and editing digital images;**
- **searching for information from a range of sources;**
- **evaluating their work;**
- **working collaboratively.**

When children are involved in creating multimedia applications they are developing a range of skills, such as:

- **using sound, text and images to communicate concepts;**
- **examining the needs of a specific audience;**
- **working collaboratively;**
- **engaging in design processes;**
- **critically evaluating their work.**

Not all multimedia applications are equal, however. There is a hierarchy of stages when developing children's own understanding of multimedia. As the children gain confidence and understanding with multimedia, the complexity of their work will grow. The simplest form, and an obvious starting point, is Type I, a linear presentation.

Type I

A linear presentation where each slide, or page, of information leads directly to the next. Some websites work in this way, taking their visitors on a 'walk' through the facilities they offer, introducing them to different aspects along the route. (See Fig. 6.5.)

Figure 6.5. Linear presentation

Teaching example 6.7

Year 5
ICT learning intention: to use presentation software to create a linear multimedia book.

Literacy learning intention: to write for a specific audience.

The teacher engaged the Year 5 children in creating multimedia books for a specific audience: Year 1. The children undertook some simple research to find favourite subjects for Year 1 readers. Then they planned their book. After considering the needs of their 'target audience' the majority of the children chose to write short stories based on animal characters. Simple storyboards were developed between the paired children. Then the children composed the story using Textease word processor. As the story took shape the children also produced a number of images, some chose to use a software paint package, others drew illustrations on paper and then captured them digitally with a scanner.

Once the story and the artwork was complete, the children turned the separate page elements into a simple linked presentation by adding hyperlink buttons to connect each page to the subsequent one.

The teacher had chosen Textease as a platform for the children to produce their book because the Textease word processor and presentation tools are very similar. Therefore the children could easily utilise skills they had already practised while working on this new project.

Type 2 *nursery rhyme*

A linear presentation (Type 1) is pure narrative: one element literally following another as in a traditional tale. Type 2 can best be thought of as analogous to a reference book. Each page of information has a potential appendix, a footnote of additional information. The hyperlinks enable the reader to 'jump' directly to this additional information. This type of presentation is useful as a way of offering definition for specific terms, or as a way of giving further information regarding a particular image or phrase. In web terminology the main series of slides can be thought of as parent slides and the sub-slides as child slides. The child slide usually links back to the parent slide so that after a reader has 'jumped' to the additional information they can quickly return to their place before moving on. The image below (Figure 6.6) represents a simple narrative presentation with three hyperlinked child slides, each offering additional information. In some presentations it may be desirable for the child slides to have additional child slides of their own. The main route, the narrative structure, however, still remains within the presentation as a strong spine out of which the additional slides are accessed. Many commercial websites present information in this way; each main page offers an overview of the product or item with a link to additional information, further images or ordering details.

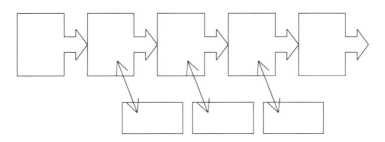

Figure 6.6. Presentation with links

Teaching example 6.8

Year 4/5

ICT learning intention: to use hyperlinks to create a presentation using parent–child pages.

History learning intention: to identify the main features in a Roman settlement.

This project was part of a history focus on the Romans in Britain. The intention was to produce a class presentation that other children could use to find out about the Romans. Although the history element was an important feature the class teacher wanted the children to investigate different ways of producing presentations first. Therefore, to begin this project the teacher shared with the children a number of PowerPoint presentations created by previous children in the class. The children accessed and explored them for part of a teaching session. The teacher encouraged them to work through them to familiarise themselves with the structure and the focus of the presentations. She asked them to note some of the design features and to discuss how the presentations could be improved. They were asked to think about questions such as these.

- Was the text a good size?
- Was the font used readable and appropriate?
- Were colours used well: did they enhance the text and images, or did they interfere and detract?
- Was there a balance and feel of style to all of the slides?
- Were transitions used well, or did they interfere with the slides?
- Had the creators of the presentation considered their audience?
- Was animation used purposefully, or was it irritating?

The teacher then explained that they would be using the information they had found together with the class work they had done on the Romans to form a presentation. The children shared their findings and then explored ways of making effective presentations. Together with the teacher they arrived at the idea of having a main page with an image of the Roman settlement. This would contain a number of hyperlinks to a set of 'child' pages, each offering additional information (Fig. 6.7).

.

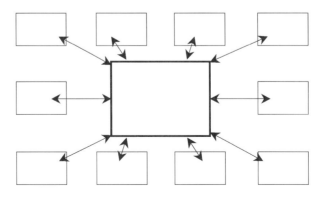

Figure 6.7. Hyperlinks

The children worked in small groups; each group used research material they had been collecting as part of the project to write and illustrate one of the 'child' slides. One group created the main, introductory slide. This slide consisted of images and hyperlinks. The teacher demonstrated ways of making hotspot hyperlinks from this main image and the children worked together to complete all of the links.

Reflective task

With an activity of this nature, think about the kind of support the children would need. How could you offer differentiated support for the children with weaker ICT skills?

This kind of activity is very effective since the children are fully involved in the design process. Clear ICT skills are being developed, but there are also links to design and technology areas.

Type 3

This style of multimedia presentation offers a full range of alternatives to the user; each individual slide may have multiple hyperlinks to other slides. These hyperlinks will be to additional child slides, or they can equally well be to another slide with further links. No traditional 'narrative' spine exists here as the different parts of the presentation are broken into sub-elements (see Figure 6.8).

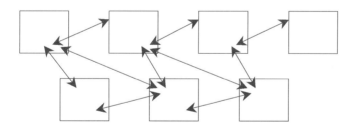

Figure 6.8. Presentation with multiple alternatives

This is the most versatile of all arrangements and is the one most often used by large websites. The user has access to almost any slide within the application from any other section. The difficulty of such a system however is the possibility of users getting lost in the maze of pages and links. It is essential, therefore, to have a method of clearly navigating the pages. Without clear navigation users could become easily frustrated attempting to locate specific elements.

This type of application is less useful as a form of directly presenting information; it is more effective as a response to individual needs and interests. The format is most often used as part of individual learning packages in which children can choose particular pathways through the application according to their needs and interests.

Children can be introduced to this format through the idea of a multi-ending adventure story. The web of links between slides can represent the number of choices open to characters; the hyperlinks acting as decision points that are available to the reader at each slide. An alternative would be to emulate an information website where children design slides with links to additional information and also offer a clear navigational path through the material for visitors. For example, the following account describes how a teacher gave a Year 6 class the challenge of designing linked web pages for their school's website.

Teaching example 6.9

Year 6

ICT learning intention: to use a web authoring package to create a series of linked pages as part of the school's web site.

Geography learning intention: to identify and describe the main features of Whitby town.

Following a residential visit to the coastal town of Whitby, the class were challenged to produce a series of web pages detailing their experiences. The focus of this was as a way of informing parents and other children in school what they did during their week's stay. While on the visit the children had taken a large number of digital images and also recorded sounds from different parts of the town; these, together with written elements, were to form the basis of their web pages.

Initially, the teacher discussed the project with the children and asked them to decide which areas of the visit they wanted to focus on and possible ideas for the structure of the pages. As a starting point the children were asked to look at a range of local information websites concentrating on effective page design, colour, layout, style and text size. They were also asked to consider other features.

- **How easy is the site to navigate?**
- **How appropriate are the images (not enough, too many, too large, too small)?**
- **Is the style and content suited to the intended audience?**

From the initial discussion on the content of the web pages, the teacher organised the children into groups which focused on the following ideas:

- **a virtual tour of Whitby;**
- **images of the geographical features;**
- **images of the residential accommodation;**
- **information about the wildlife;**
- **fishing and the history of fishing in Whitby;**
- **a diary of the week's stay.**

Following these discussions each group of children prepared a paper plan of their web pages, focusing on the layout and how their pages would link to each other.

In the following session the teacher used an IWB to demonstrate creating and saving simple pages with Microsoft FrontPage. Each group then began to develop their pages. This work took place over a number of sessions.

For activities of this nature, where children work as a group within the main task, you may find it necessary to have a different learning intention for each group.

This last example clearly relies on the children's and the teacher's knowledge of ICT and confidence with the use of web-authoring software. It also relies heavily on the nature of the school's facilities and the software available. It is worth bearing in mind that this kind of project may not be possible in all settings with all children.

Practical task

Consider a recent school where you were placed. Did the children have the confidence and skills to work on an extended ICT project?

Did the school have the technological resources to effectively support such an activity? If not, think how you could adapt a project like this for schools or classes where:

- *the ICT skills are less secure, or*
- *the school resources are less effective?*

Reflective task

Identify a topic in your future teaching where it would be appropriate to have pupils create a multimedia presentation, then:

- *Note some key learning objectives you would hope to achieve by having pupils using or creating a multimedia presentation.*
- *Identify the kinds of information you would want your children to locate for the activity.*
- *Outline the skills the children will need to successfully implement multimedia work.*

This chapter has outlined four ways in which multimedia applications can be used in classrooms to both extend ICT knowledge and support learning across the curriculum. Each enhances teaching and enables the introduction of concepts, the sharing of ideas, and the demonstration of skills. On your visits to schools you may have seen teachers using multimedia in each of the identified ways.

Multimedia communication in practice:
a summary of key points

_____ *Multimedia is a mix of images, sound, video, animation and text.*

_____ *Multimedia can be used in a range of ways:*

-- by the teacher as a demonstration tool;

-- by the teacher and children together to extend learning;

-- by the children to focus on specific skills;

-- by children developing their own multimedia applications.

_____ *By incorporating multimedia into their work children can extend their communication skills.*

References

Fleming, N. D. (2001) *Teaching and learning styles: VARK strategies.* Honolulu: VARK-Learn Publications.

OFSTED (2005) *Primary National Strategy: an evaluation of its impact in primary schools 2004/05.* London: HMSO.

QCA (1998) *A scheme of work for key stages l and 2: information technology.* London: QCA Publications.

QCA (2000) *Curriculum guidance for the foundation stage.* London: QCA.

QCA (2005) *A curriculum for the future: subjects consider the challenge.* London: QCA.

Further reading

Pritchard, A. (2005) *Ways of learning: learning theories and learning styles in the classroom.* London: David Fulton. This book offers a detailed introduction to many of the major theories about children's learning styles. The author examines how to develop effective learning situations, and how to plan and create the best opportunities for successful, lasting learning across all curriculum areas.

Resources

Happy Pet is an interactive online activity which is part of BBC Wales' Bobinogs education site. www.bbc.co.uk/wales/bobinogs/games/gamespage.shtml.

Mouse Music interactive CD ROM published by d2 digital by design. Further information in available from www.d2digital.co.uk.

Fizzy's First Numbers from Sherston Software Ltd. www.sherston.com.

Crocodile Clips freely available from www.crocodile-clips.com/education/.

7 ICT STRATEGIES: MULTIMEDIA COMMUNICATION

By the end of this chapter you should:

- have knowledge and understanding of the broad nature of multimedia;
- be aware of the range of ways in which ICT can support subject learning;
- recognise and use the motivational advantages of using multimedia applications;
- be aware of the different stages of complexity within multimedia applications;
- be able to reflect on your own practice and identify areas for development;
- be able to plan and organise learning in creative ways to enable children to share, present and exchange text using ICT;
- be able to suggest ways of differentiating written communication activities with ICT;
- be aware of possible ways of assessing children's ICT capability;
- be able to identify issues of health and safety in ICT.

Professional Standards for QTS
Q2.1, Q2.2, Q2.3, Q2.4, Q2.5, Q2.6, Q3.3, Q3.4, Q3.5

Links to the Foundation Stage Guidance and the National Curriculum

In the Foundation Stage children will use information communication technology to support their learning.

At Key Stage 1 children will gather information from a variety of sources and share their ideas by presenting information in a variety of forms (1a, 3a). Children will also work with a range of information to investigate the different ways it can be presented, explore a variety of ICT tools and talk about the uses of ICT outside and inside school (5a, 5b, 5c).

At Key Stage 2 children will prepare information for development using ICT, share and exchange information in a variety of forms, think carefully about the content when communicating information (1b, 3a, 3b). Throughout their work children should work with others to explore a variety of information sources, and be involved in investigating and comparing the uses of ICT inside and outside school (5b, 5c).

Introduction

Multimedia is a very powerful form of communication, a form that surrounds us and, to some extent, shapes the way we think. We live in a world where much of the information we receive comes to us through multimedia: interactive DVDs, TV broadcasts and internet sites all use the full range of media to offer us information. Mobile phones offered text as a rapid way of communicating, and now images and video can be used alongside the text (or in place of it) to refine and enhance any message. This is very powerful, and any teaching or learning that embodies such a mixed media is automatically enhanced. However, the communication developments of using such a variety (sound, images, animation and video) still have their roots in the textual forms of communications discussed in Part 3.

At the Foundation Stage pupils are involved in using ICT to support their learning and at this stage children will be becoming familiar with the numerous technical devices available in everyday life and how they help us carry out everyday tasks, things such as mobile phones, talking books etc. The Curriculum Guidance indicates that pupils need to experience a range of media such as *CD ROMs, audio and visual reference material, pictures, photographs, maps, artefacts and products* (QCA, 2000, p83).

The National Curriculum requirements that are the main focus for this kind of work are therefore the same as were discussed in Chapter 5.

Exchanging and sharing information are outlined below.

Key Stage 1

Pupils should be taught:

3a: how to share their ideas by presenting information in a variety of forms;
3b: to present their completed work effectively.

Key Stage 2

Pupils should be taught:

3a: how to share and exchange information in a variety of forms including email;
3b: to be sensitive to the needs of the audience and think carefully about the content and quality when communicating information.

Multimedia

With multimedia the focus changes slightly in that the terms 'variety of forms' from both Key Stages 1 and 2 requirements take on greater importance. The non-statutory examples [printed in square brackets in the National Curriculum documentation] indicate that this 'variety of forms' could include pupils:

- **using text, images, tables, sounds;**
- **making musical compositions;**
- **working with animation software;**
- **creating displays or posters for public display;**
- **presenting work to other pupils or for parents;**
- **publishing material on the internet.**

In the previous chapter it was suggested that multimedia could be seen in four ways: multimedia used by the teacher, the teacher and children together, the children, or children developing their own multimedia applications. Table 7.1 illustrates how the four uses offer different levels of control to the pupils and how this use of ICT supports, enhances or extends the pupil's learning.

Table 7.1. Four ways of using multimedia.

		Use	Level of control	ICT ...
1	Multimedia used by the teacher	Demonstrating and clarifying concepts	Learner has no control	... supports subject learning
2	Multimedia used by the teacher and children together	Exploring concepts or learning about multimedia	Learner has some control	... supports and enhances subject learning
3	Multimedia used by the children			
4	Children developing their own multimedia applications	Enhancing their knowledge and understanding, and refining their ICT skills	Learner has most control	... extends subject learning

The first of these ways is the notion of demonstration: multimedia is used purely as an aid to teaching and explaining. This is undoubtedly a powerful and flexible use of the technology, and it effectively supports subject learning. However, because of the nature of teaching 'demonstrations', the pupils have little or no direct control over the multimedia. This use will be discussed later (in the section Multimedia as a tool for teaching, page 100).

In the second and third ways, children have increasing control over the applications. Teaching example 6.5 described a session where children were using an interactive number application to develop their recognition of specific numerals. They were physically using the program, controlling screen elements with a mouse, so had some control, and the use of the ICT supported and enhanced their learning.

The fourth way of using multimedia was demonstrated with Teaching examples 6.6, 6.7 and 6.8. Here the pupils have greater degrees of control over the program. They are directly involved in developing presentations or multimedia applications. This is the most powerful and sophisticated use of multimedia. As Atherton has argued, *to use multimedia authoring software to combine text, images, sound, animation and video creatively to communicate understanding and to share this understanding with a wider audience is perhaps one of the most rewarding and exciting teaching experiences I have had. I also feel strongly that it is one of the most memorable and educationally empowering learning experiences that my pupils have had* (Atherton, 2002, p127).

Clearly, the skills necessary for pupils (and teachers) to utilise multimedia in this way do not develop overnight. In order for pupils to be involved in these memorable and educationally empowering experiences, a great deal of preliminary work has to be done. The remainder of this chapter will examine the skills associated with developing the confidence and ability to use multimedia effectively.

Tools and strategies

When pupils are involved in developing and creating their own multimedia applications, they are moving beyond the Exchanging and Sharing Information strand of the National Curriculum. Some of this work also relates to the Developing Ideas and Making Things Happen strand. The most relevant elements here are:

Key Stage 1

Pupils should be taught:

2a: to use text, tables images and sounds to develop their ideas;
2c: how to plan and give instructions to make things happen;
2d: to try things out and explore what happens in real and imaginary situations.

Key Stage 2

Pupils should be taught:

2a: how to develop and refine ideas by bringing together, organising and reorganising text, tables, images and sound as appropriate.

These are major strands which overlap with examples and strategies discussed in the chapters on Control (Part 6). There are also clear cross-curricular links here to design technology.

Practical task

Refer to the National Curriculum documentation for design technology and make a note of the links you can identify between the strands within that document and the ones within ICT. Think of one activity you could carry out on your next placement which would enable pupils to develop appropriate knowledge, understanding and skills from both documents.

Before pupils can successfully combine media in a multimedia application or presentation, they first need to understand the nature of each separate medium.

Text

Children work with text throughout their school life. Whether they are reading it, or producing it, ICT can extend and enhance their knowledge (see Part 3 of this book). Throughout their work, pupils are refining and developing their knowledge that text transfers meaning and that the way the text is presented can have an affect on the reader. They consider punctuation, text size, style of font, formatting and even colour. The development includes learning about different styles of writing from poetry to persuasive texts, and also an understanding and appreciation of graphic design and layout. It could be considered that text forms the backbone of multimedia, and that the other media support it. However, although text has been discussed first in this section, that is largely due to its commonality rather than its primacy. Effective multimedia presentations can be designed with limited use of text, and pupils, therefore, need to recognise that other ways of communicating messages are equally important, even if they are not as ubiquitous.

Images

Images offer a very powerful way of communicating. Most advertisements and logos depend on a graphic element to support the message. Some have little or no textual components at all. Similarly, graphic elements are important components within multimedia applications. However, it is important that pupils master the skills of creating, inserting and working with images before they are asked to use them as part of multimedia work. There also need to be planned opportunities for them to develop their understanding of what kinds of images to use, why particular images are used and their power to communicate. Again, it is useful to turn to the world of advertising as a starting point for examples of powerful images.

When children explore talking books, CD ROMs or websites they are reminded of the importance of effectively combining text and images. They also have opportunities to work directly with images in a number of different ways:

- **using ready made images such as clip art or stock photographs;**
- **creating their own images using a painting/design package;**
- **using digital photographs of areas of the school or of objects seen through a microscope.**

In the Foundation Stage children may be moving simple stock images around the screen, for example, moving an image of a frog until it is alongside an appropriate label. They may also be involved in taking photographs or using a software paint package to create pictures or patterns.

At Key Stage 1 and 2 pupils may work with mixed media images. For example, they may be involved in using a scanner to transform a painting or picture they have created into a digital image that can be used within another program.

Throughout the primary years, pupils will be developing their skills of combining images and text. Such text-image combinations may be quite rudimentary to begin with. Word processors such as Textease accept clip-art (or scanned images) easily and these can be pasted onto the text area and manipulated with ease. In other word processing packages, the use of a simple template made of a text box and an image-space may be necessary. The pupils choose an image for one side and input text beside (or beneath) it (see Figure 7.1).

My dog is called Fern. She has black and white fur on her face.

she likes to eat chees.

Figure 7.1. Using image and text

The focus is on the skills of copying and pasting (or inserting) images, and the correct combination of appropriate text with the image. For short, tightly focused activities the pupils could be:

- **sorting images and labelling them;**
- **designing a 'Wanted' poster;**
- **advertising a house for sale;**
- **creating an illustrated dictionary of topic words;**
- **listing the attributes of a 2-D or 3-D shape;**
- **describing a holiday location, a member of their family or a pet;**
- **describing a minibeast they photographed.**

Pupils should also be encouraged to look at existing designs where images and text have been combined. This can be through looking at picture books, magazines, web pages or existing multimedia applications. Figure 7.2 clearly illustrates the effectiveness of clear layout of images and text.

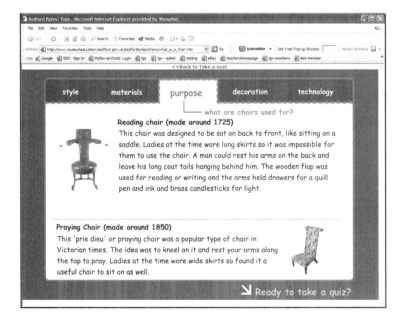

Figure 7.2. What is a Chair? is part of an online interactive resource from Bedford Borough Council.

Once the skills of inserting and using images appropriately have been mastered, pupils can begin to develop them further through the appropriate use of multiple images and text styles. The QCA Unit 3A (Combining Text and Graphics) has a final, integrated task where pupils are involved in producing a class magazine. In this, the pupils can explore and utilise a greater range of font styles, text sizes and images that would suit a specific audience.

Later in Key Stage 2, pupils could further develop this work by using more sophisticated graphic design features of paint packages; using brush, pen and selection tools, learning about the use of colour, pattern, contrast, tone and hue. There are specific cross-curricular links here with the art curriculum and design technology.

Reflective task

Recall when you last worked with pupils using paint or drawing software. What were your learning intentions? Was the focus of the work the development of ICT skills or the understanding of design elements such as tone, colour or pattern? Would it have been possible to adapt the learning intentions to focus on both areas?

Sound

Pupils work with sound whenever they:

- **record their stories using cassette or digital recorders;**
- **interact with the sound facilities of a talking book or talking word processor;**
- **listen to music played on a record player, tape recorder, CD ROM, or to music that has been stored digitally;**
- **explore aspects of music using composition software;**
- **rearrange icons representing musical phrases to compose simple tunes;**
- **use electronic keyboards or other MIDI devices to combine sequences of sounds;**
- **record and communicate musical ideas.**

Many of these activities will be planned as part of cross-curricular work with music. Others can be linked through speaking and listening objectives, most of these will occur as part of role play, drama work or when pupils are involved in hot-seat activities or mock interviews. Whatever the context of the learning, pupils should begin to develop an understanding of how sounds can be made, recorded, adapted and used. While much of this focus will be on developing the ICT skills to work with digitally recorded sounds, it is also important that pupils are encouraged to think carefully about the types of sounds they are using. This is developing their knowledge and appreciation of the way music, sounds and sound effects can communicate meaning. They should be thinking about the appropriateness of the sounds they choose and the needs of their audience. This will enable them to move from the notion of working with sounds in isolation to the multimedia concept of working with sounds tied to another medium. The sound-message should complement and enhance the message delivered in the other media. It is also possible to tie short (clearly focused)

projects together: pupils may use images and sounds, or text and sounds. Any of the examples listed in the Images section, above, could be enhanced by the addition of appropriate sound elements.

Some schools (Downs CE Primary or AceKids, for example – see the Resources section at the end of this chapter) are now experimenting with communication means that use sound to the exclusion of all other media. This is the use of podcasts. Pupils prepare short 'radio' style programmes, often using a simple script describing, for example, the activities the school has undertaken during the term. This is then read aloud and recorded digitally before being turned into an audio file for transmission over the web. Other children within the school, parents, members of the school community, and the wider world can then access the podcast 'radio-show' to learn about the school's activities. Clearly, having such a global audience offers the pupils a very motivating and meaningful context for their work. The development of a podcast also offers the pupils the opportunity to develop their teamwork, enterprise, technical literacy and planning skills. Many elements of this are very effective, since pupils are involved in thinking about the nature of the audience, planning and preparing the material.

Without a meaningful context and clear learning intentions, 'sound' is a more difficult medium to explore than text or images. It is all too easy to use sound technology as a way of simply 'recording' prepared transcripts. This is akin to the early misuses which word-processing software suffered: used as a way of presenting work. The full versatility of the ICT (sound recording equipment, in this case) is not fully utilised.

Animation

Animation has a number of different meanings within multimedia work. The first and simplest is the use of movement to introduce a screen element within a presentation. This is usually used to make text or images fly, slid or spin into view as part of a PowerPoint presentation. The use and application of such movements is usually easy to accomplish. The harder aspect is in encouraging pupils (and some adults) to use restraint when applying these effects. The pupils need time to play and experiment to see what each effect will do and how it looks to an audience. They then need encouragement to use the effects judiciously.

Reflective task

Prepare a presentation which deliberately overuses the full range of text animation effects. Demonstrate the presentation to pupils or other students, then ask for their opinion. This is a useful way to start a discussion regarding the effective use of animation and similar effects in a presentation.

Working with animation can bring enthusiasm to a multimedia project. The pupils can be involved in using stop frame animation; this is when separate images of an object are combined into a sequence so that it appears as if it is one continuous action.

The second form of animation which pupils can work with is 'stop-motion' animation, or claymation. This is the technique where multiple images are created, each is slightly different and when the images are viewed in rapid succession the impression of movement is created. For children who have grown up with animated features such as *Pingu* or *Wallace and Gromit* the ability to accomplish something similar is very motivating and meaningful.

Using a digital camera or a web camera, and suitable software (Digital Video and a movie editor or istopmotion from Boinx software, for example), pupils can cause any object to appear to move. Again, as with animated text effects, it is useful to give the pupils time to experiment with any object. The simplest practice sessions can utilise items that are close at hand: a dancing computer mouse, or paperclips performing a synchronised swimming ballet as they cross the area of an A4 piece of paper.

Once pupils are familiar with the techniques, it is also possible for them to work with models made from pipe cleaners, silver foil, construction kits or modelling clay. In this way, even simple animations provide a very useful motivation for children developing their story telling. Animation activities can be used across all areas of the curriculum, but they have specific links with design technology, art, music and literacy. They are also very good examples of long-term projects; these activities cannot be completed in a short space of time. Teaching sessions need to be well planned, but flexible, in order for the pupils to make the most gains with this type of activity.

A typical timeframe is seven or eight separate teaching sessions, as illustrated in Table 7.2.

Table 7.2. Typical teaching timeframe

Session content	Focus
One session focusing on the story	Literacy
Two sessions to design and build the models and the scenery	Design technology/art
One session working with the models to produce a story board	Literacy
Two sessions to film the animation	ICT
One session viewing the film and designing music	Music
One session to make any adjustments to the film and add music, sound effects and titles	ICT

Useful strategies:

- **Remind the pupils that the narrative is still the most important element.**
- **Encourage the pupils to break their storyline into scenes and to decide how long each scene should be.**
- **Plan the scenes and include ideas about shots, camera angles and framing.**
- **Think about the design of their characters; can they make each one uniquely identifiable?**

- Think about the use of colour. Use a contrasting colour for the background so that the characters are easy to see.
- Encourage the pupils to think about how their characters will move. For example, is it necessary to have legs?
- Give the pupils time and encouragement so they can be truly inventive when designing and building their models.

Working on animation projects can encourage language development and allow logical, spatial, collaborative and creative skills to flourish. Animation development is a cross-curricular classroom activity that challenges the creative talents of pupils.

Multimedia as a tool for learning (putting it all together)

Each medium, text, image, sound and animation has been considered separately. Clearly, when we ask pupils to utilise multimedia software to combine these elements there is no expectation that they will need to address all of them, that they need to employ them in a particular order or that they should be seen as discrete elements. Pupils need experience and understanding of working with these, and other, media first. This way, when it comes to working with a multimedia package they already have the skills and capabilities to select the most appropriate media-tool to use and are not restricted because of their lack of skills. This is important because when working on a history presentation (for example) the children will be extending and enhancing their knowledge of history, and do not need the burden of uncertainty with the ICT to prevent them from fully utilising all aspects of multimedia to further their historical learning. As Lachs (1999) has suggested, *when we ask [pupils] to design and make multimedia packages in other subjects we are making qualitatively different demands on their learning of that subject – that the production process of making multimedia artefacts affects the way the learn about subject content.* (Lachs, 1999, p12)

Multimedia presentations enable pupils to unite previous learning and usually involve them in working collaboratively. In a number of cases, teachers suggest that pupils work as an editorial team, each with a different role, often the pupils give their team a name and create a group identity.

PowerPoint or Textease are both powerful multimedia applications which adults and children can use. However, there is a range of other multimedia programs available.

- *Junior MultiMedia Lab* can be used to help Key Stage 2 pupils create multimedia presentations of a high standard, using sound, animation, pictures and movie clips.
- *Hyperstudio* enables Key Stages I and 2 pupils to create a range of multimedia presentations.
- *2Create* enables Key Stages I and 2 children to to develop their writing and presentation skills as they develop a range of multimedia presentations.

- *2Animate!* can be customised to suit individual pupils' needs and enables them to make simple animations that can be printed out, saved or uploaded to a website.

Teaching example 6.8 described how a number of children from a mixed class of Year 4 and Year 5 pupils worked together to produce a presentation on the Romans in Britain. The work, however, was split into the following sections:

1. Examining a range of existing presentations.
2. Evaluating some of the design features of the presentations (see page 84).
3. Using this information to help design their own presentation.
4. Working in small groups to produce the necessary slides.
5. Combining the slides to create the presentation.

This series of activities (spread over a number of teaching sessions) highlighted the design process and strengthened the children's understanding of design as well as enabling them to develop their ICT capabilities.

The format of the presentation, a main (parent) slide, represented by the larger rectangle in Figure 6.7 (see page 84), with a series of secondary (child) slides, is very flexible.

The same initial design can be used as a template for a range of different presentations:

- **The main introductory slide can be a group photograph of the children. Hotspots are placed over each child so that when they are selected (clicked) the user is taken to a secondary slide with more information about that particular child.**

- **The main slide can be a plan of the school. Each room is linked to a child-slide with further information.**

- **The main slide could be a scanned image of a pupil's treasure island painting. Elements on the map (palm trees, caves, sandy coves, etc) are linked to child-slides. These child-slides could offer detailed geographical information, or be sections of an adventure story. An alternative approach could be to turn the presentation into a treasure hunt game: one child-slide bears a picture of a treasure box; the remaining slides contain more negative elements such as images of sharks or text announcing 'Bad luck!'**

Children who are familiar with working with hotspots and hyperlinks as part of multimedia presentations will be able to work with web authoring packages in a very similar way. Most multimedia programs have the facility to save the presentation that has been created as a series of linked web pages and this means that it is possible for children to be involved in designing and working on school websites.

Multimedia as a tool for teaching

A multimedia application enables teachers to demonstrate concepts dynamically. The automated movement or changing colours can help to illustrate things that are otherwise not easily discussed or described. For example, in Figure 7.3 the Flash animation from BBC Science Clips is designed to describe the orbit of the Earth around the Sun. Pupils can see how the Earth and Moon move in a given amount of time. The animation simplifies the explanation of this complex concept. The multiple movements within this image (the Moon traces its orbit around the Earth as the Earth orbits the Sun) are quite complex and would otherwise be difficult to reproduce.

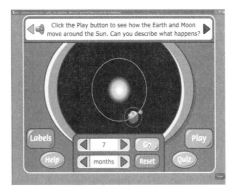

Figure 7.3 BBC Science Clips (see Resources, p104)

This type of multimedia is effective and purposeful. As was discussed in Chapter 6, it is an application of good teaching and learning practices. Effective teachers have always used visual aids, like washing lines, paper cut-outs, coloured chalk and pens or puppets, to support their teaching. Multimedia applications should be seen as an extension of these teaching aids, not a replacement.

Figure 7.4 is another example from BBC Science Clips. This light and shadow demonstration uses multimedia to help clarify many concepts. Many elements within the demonstration software can be manipulated: the light can be moved higher or lower, it can be brought closer or moved further away; the object in the path of the light can also be changed.

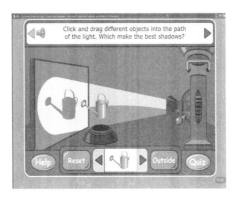

Figure 7.4 BBC Science Clips (see Resources, p104)

This allows pupils to see and discuss the effects the changes have on the shadow produced by the light. As a starting point for discussion, or as a tool for assessing a pupil's understanding of light and shadow, this is effective. However, it is clearly not a replacement for first hand experience. Pupils using real torches, creating and investigating real shadows would gain far more than with this. Unlike the Earth in space example, the concepts here are easier to demonstrate without the multimedia.

The IWB is a technology that has arrived at a time that the notion of multiple intelligences has gained in popularity. Some software attempts to combine the two, but it can be argued that sliding images on a IWB is not particularly kinaesthetic. Similarly the addition of a random sound effect to a PowerPoint presentation can be more an irritant than an aid to learning. It is important to remember that the motivation factor of multimedia is not inherent in the software itself. Many people have sat through bad multimedia presentations and wished they were elsewhere; the use of animation, sound effects and flashy colours did nothing to improve the actual content. The use of ICT will not automatically make a bad teaching session good. Nor will the injection of an IWB mean that learning is suddenly improved.

When using multimedia to demonstrate teaching points, then, it is important to be clear what the teaching points are. Similarly, it is important to choose the correct multimedia tool. Many educational CD ROMs can be used to demonstrate specific subject matter, Flash animations, or presentations can be used over the internet. A number of educational websites also offer presentations which can be downloaded. iwb.org.uk, for example, offers a good range of free resources created for teachers who are using an IWB.

As has already been discussed, multimedia has the potential to interest and motivate. When teachers use multimedia to demonstrate or explain they are using these factors, plus the appreciation that animation and video can make concepts easier to understand. Elements such as these are most effective as an introduction to new concepts: the beginning of a history or science topic, for example, or as part of a numeracy or literacy whole class teaching session.

It is possible for you to create your own multimedia presentation; this will mean that the content is perfectly matched to the needs of the pupils and the requirements of the curriculum.

Professional issues

Planning and organisation

The application of multimedia as a teaching tool needs to be carefully planned for. The learning intentions need to be clear and the presentation needs to match the focus of the session. Ensure that the multimedia is offering an advantage to either yourself or the pupils. If it clarifies or eases an explanation, or if it makes your work more efficient then it has a place. If, however, it only adds superficial decoration then do not use it.

If you are using an IWB with pupils it is useful if you can plan to familiarise them with the workings of the board and its tools as suggested below.

- **Plan for whole-class and small group activities, so that more children can have more time working at the board.**
- **Encourage all children to take part in whole-class sessions by asking the children to use an imaginary 'air pen' to demonstrate moving objects or using tools.**
- **Encourage children to use programs on the board during child-initiated activities.**
- **Display and use key vocabulary, such as: pen, highlighter, rubber, mouse, click, double click, tool, icon.**

When the pupils are involved in multimedia authoring, remember that it will take a considerable amount of time. All the elements need careful planning and the pupils need to have had experience of using the media elements separately first. It is often far better to work with a number of small (successful) presentations rather than involving the children in a hugely complicated and never finished multimedia extravaganza. The children will need to work collaboratively and will also need time to prepare elements of their work away from the computers. These are important considerations and should be specifically planned for, as shown below.

- **Involve the pupils in working as a team, each individual with a specific role.**
- **Plan opportunities for the pupils to design the presentation on paper. Encourage them to share their ideas and to only move to work on the multimedia application once the design process and all their ideas are clear.**
- **Involve children in real life problems, set up by them, and planned and logged by the computer.**
- **Organise a series of open-ended projects and ask the pupils to complete a timetable in order to plan how they will work on each task.**

Monitoring and assessing

When children are involved in designing and creating multimedia presentations they are learning that computer applications:

- include a range of media;
- provide a range of options.

This ICT knowledge and understanding should be assessed alongside the skills they have developed. These skills may include (for example), the ability to:

- **design multimedia pages;**
- **diagram the links between pages;**
- **create button hyperlinks, text hyperlinks or hotspots to link pages;**
- **work with and develop images;**
- **sample sounds.**

Since much of the work will be collaborative it is important to observe the processes involved in order to assess the children's development. It is not always possible to identify what contribution each child may or may not have made from the finished presentation. It is also useful to engage the children in their own assessment. One solution to this, and as a way of further involving children in their own assessment is to encourage the children to maintain their own 'I can do...' type records. Table 7.3 is a useful example since it acknowledges that the children will undertake some of the work together.

Table 7.3. 'I can do ...' record

Multimedia		
Skills I have learnt with the rest of my class		
• I know what multimedia is and how it can be used		
• I helped to choose a topic for our multimedia work		
• I helped to plan our multimedia work		
Skills I have practised by myself. I can ...		
• Load multimedia software		
• Alter the way my work looks		
• Add images to my work		
• Add clipart to my work		
• Record and add sounds and sound effects to my work		
• Add already recorded sounds to my work		
• Use preset animation effects		
• Add new animation		
• Link screens together		
• Use special effects to move between screens		
• Save my work		
• Print my work		
• I have helped prepare a multimedia project for a particular audience		
• I have presented a project to a particular group of people		

ICT strategies: multimedia communication:

a summary of key points

___ The National Curriculum sets out requirements for ICT regarding the knowledge and understanding which pupils should be taught.

___ Multimedia work should be seen as cross-curricular.

___ By incorporating multimedia into their work children can extend their communication skills.

___ Multimedia offers considerable benefits to learning and teaching:

-- it can be used as an aid to clarifying concepts;

-- when pupils are involved in using multimedia authoring packages it can extend and enhance their learning in cross-curricular subjects.

___ It is important for pupils to have had experience of working with and developing the use of individual media before they are asked to work with multimedia applications.

References

Atherton, T (2002) in Loveless, A. and Dore, B. (eds) *ICT in the primary school: learning and teaching with information and communications technology.* Buckingham: OUP.

Lachs, V. (1999) in Sefton-Green, J. (ed.) *Young people, creativity and the new technologies: the challenge of digital arts.* London: Routledge Falmer.

QCA (2000) *Curriculum guidance for the Foundation Stage.* London: QCA.

Further reading

Loveless, A. and Dore, B. (eds) *ICT in the primary school: learning and teaching with information and communications technology.* Buckingham: OUP. This book discusses many of the ways in which ICT can make a critical contribution to children's learning. The authors suggest that ICT's potential to enable children to show and gain knowledge is dependent upon the teachers' understanding of the purposes of learning and the ways in which learners, teachers and new technologies can interact with each other.

Resources

BBC Science Clips. http://www.bbc.co.uk/schools/scienceclips/ages/7-8/ light_shadows.shtml. and http://www.bbc.co.uk/schools/scienceclips/ages/9-10/ earth_sun_moon.shtml

Interactive Whiteboard Resources. www.iwb.org.uk.

Interactive resource from Bedford Borough Council. www.museumeducation.bedford.gov.uk/bedfordbytes.

Istopmotion from Boinx. Further details from http://istopmotion.com.

2Animate! and **2Create** from 2Simple Software. Further details from www.2simple.com.

Hyperstudio from Sunburst technologies. Further details from www.taglearning.com.

Junior MultiMedia Lab from Sherston. Further details from www.sherston.com.

Downs CE Primary podcasts. Full details from www.downsfm.com.

AceKids podcasts. Full details from www.adrianbruce.com/acekids/index.htm.

8 REVIEWING, MODIFYING AND EVALUATING IN PRACTICE

By the end of this chapter you should:

- *be aware of where 'reviewing, modifying and evaluating' fits within the curriculum;*
- *be aware of the starting points for reviewing, modifying and evaluating;*
- *understand the importance of collaborative work for developing reviewing, modifying and evaluating skills;*
- *understand how provisionality can ease the way in which children respond to reviewing, modifying and evaluating;*
- *be aware of the progressive nature of reviewing, modifying and evaluating;*
- *appreciate the range of ways in which ICT can support subject learning.*

Professional Standards for QTS
Q2.1, Q2.2, Q2.4, Q2.6, Q3.5

Links to the Foundation Stage Guidance and the National Curriculum

In the Foundation Stage children will use information communication technology to support their learning.

At Key Stage 1 children will review what they have done to help them develop their ideas, describe the effects of their actions and talk about what they might change in future work (4a, 4b, 4c). Children will also work with a range of information to investigate the different ways it can be presented, explore a variety of ICT tools and talk about the uses of ICT outside and inside school (5a, 5b, 5c).

At Key Stage 2 children will review what they and others have done to help them develop their ideas, describe and talk about the effectiveness of their work with ICT, comparing it with other methods and considering the effect it has on others (4a, 4b), and talk about how they could improve future work. Throughout their work, children should work with others to explore a variety of information sources, and be involved in investigating and comparing the uses of ICT inside and outside school.

Introduction

Reviewing, modifying and evaluating are clearly ongoing and developing elements of all teaching and learning. Throughout every project children should be able to evaluate their work and describe how they could improve it. However, this self-reflec-tion will not happen automatically. Some children are easily satisfied with their own work, especially if they have not been fully motivated to produce it in the first place. Others can be overly self-critical to the point of rarely finishing or starting pieces of work for fear of making a mistake. Clearly there is a middle path, but most children (and adults) may not find it without some guidance.

From their earliest times in school, all children's work needs to be valued, with the teacher focusing on the positive elements. Effective, purposeful interaction with the pupil is vital.

Practical task

Consider the following teacher interaction with a child. Which of these is most effective in engaging the child in the learning process? Which one is modelling the beginnings of evaluation?

'Oh what a lovely picture, have you written your name on the back and tidied the table?'
'Wow, what a great model – and look, it's time for play.'
'That's a superb pattern. I like the shapes you've used. Why did you choose to use pentagons?'

Reflective task

Consider the ways in which you have responded to children's work in the past. Have you fully exploited the interactions in order to engage the child in the evaluation process?

Children need to be encouraged through discussion to identify for themselves what they feel they are proud of in their work and what they feel they have done well. As children gain in confidence and experience, teachers can gradually introduce opportu-nities where children are invited to suggest ways in which their own work could be developed or refined. In the Foundation Stage Curriculum Guidance these processes are not specifically connected with ICT. As learning in the Early Years is holistic these skills are mainly evident within the Early Learning Goals for Personal, Social and Emotional Development. The Curriculum Guidance indicates that children should:

- **have a developing awareness of their own needs, views and feelings and be sensitive to the needs, views and feelings of others;**
- **consider the consequences of their words and actions for themselves and others;**
- **understand that people have different needs, views, cultures and beliefs, that need to be treated with respect.**

(QCA, 2000, pp34–42)

There is also a related element in the Knowledge and Understanding of the World area of learning. Here, children should be developing an awareness, and a confidence to share, their own preferences; including 'dislike' as a way of offering a negative opinion.

- **Find out about their environment and talk about those features they like and dislike.** (QCA, 2000, p96)

A large proportion of this work within the Foundation Stage will clearly be encountered through discussion. However, specific learning opportunities should also be planned for and these will be discussed later.

At Key Stage I the National Curriculum requirements for ICT specifically mention reviewing, modifying and evaluating. Here, the requirements state that pupils should:

4a. review what they have done to help them develop their ideas;
4b. describe the effects of their actions;
4c. talk about what they might change in future work.

At Key Stage 2 the National Curriculum requirements for ICT (Reviewing, Modifying and Evaluating) state that pupils should:

4a. review what they and others have done to help them develop their ideas;
4b. describe and talk about the effectiveness of their work with ICT, comparing it with other methods and considering the effect it has on others;
4c. talk about how they could improve future work.

As with younger children, the notion of reviewing and modifying is initially supported by teacher intervention. Without this input and questioning, children may not see the need to be reflective, or develop any effective reviewing skills. This is a slightly different approach to teacher-questioning. The teacher is not just asking questions as a way of assessing the child's ability but is also modelling the process of reviewing, modifying and evaluating work as it progresses.

Foundation Stage

Effective use of ICT can help children to organise and communicate their understanding more effectively in a range of ways across all areas of learning.

Children using simple CD ROM programs, for example, are happy to use the patience of the computer to try and try again. Here ICT is a way of offering repetition of an activity in a motivating way. Children learn that icons on screen carry out instructions once pressed. Children learn to associate mouse movements with the movements of the cursor on the screen. Children can choose a screen element to activate it (in a talking book for example) and then choose it again a few moments later and (usually) the same action occurs as a result. Children learn that ICT is patient and will accept and then reaccept instructions.

Teaching example 8.1

Reception
ICT learning intention: to accurately use the mouse to select screen icons.

Literacy learning intention: to read and recognise initial and final phonemes in C-V-C words.

The teacher had been working with a group of children to develop their ability to recognise initial and final phonemes in C-V-C words. The children were introduced to the Farmer Rumtum's Letter Fun CD ROM. The teacher set up the CD so that the children could access an activity which would give them opportunities to practise identifying a series of initial and final phonemes. The children worked in pairs to identify and use the appropriate letter string. When they were successful the program responded with praise. At times some of their choices were incorrect and the program offered them another opportunity. The children gradually became more confident at recognising written and final phonemes. They had been able to practise their words several times and the fun, interactive nature of the program had maintained their enthusiasm.

ICT is often cited as being powerful because of its motivational aspect; elements of this have been discussed before in the sections on multimedia (Chapter 6). However, in this activity (and many others) the key ICT feature which supports the children's learning is 'provisionality'; that is the ability to accept changes and modifications. Watercolours applied to paper are irremovable. Handwriting with an ink pen is permanent. With ICT, however, this level of permanence only exists after work has been printed. Until that point anything and everything can be changed, adapted, remodelled, edited and re-edited as often as the user wishes. The ICT application in the above Teaching example offered more than a motivational series of images and animated characters. It offered repeated opportunities to practise identifying letter strings, and it did so in an environment where the children felt secure. The images and animation were motivating, but the provisionality ensured the children felt comfortable with the task.

Teaching example 8.2

Reception
ICT learning intention: to use 'click and drag' to move icons into selected positions.

Creative development learning intention: to create a simple repeating pattern.

The class had been discussing and working with repeating patterns. The teacher asked the children to produce a pattern using repeated elements. A small group of children worked with the stamp tools in the painting program Kid Pix (from Research Machines).

The children quickly filled the blank screen with images, deleted them and refilled the screen, experimenting and judging the results until they found one they thought worth printing out. The teacher discussed the work with the children and encouraged them to talk about their patterns and their designs. She encouraged the children to demonstrate and explain how they had operated the mouse and how they had directed the stamp icons around the screen.

She was also keen to encourage them to state what they liked about the patterns and why they were effective. She also encouraged the children to think how they might change this pattern, would they have preferred a wider choice of stamps/icons to use?

Young children can be easily satisfied with their work, and many want to see an image printed out. For them a picture is not 'theirs' unless they can hold it in their hand. In this example the teacher used the pupils' interest in the printed work; she made the point of printing the image and then taking it back to the screen so the pupil could compare the work on paper with the image on the screen. The teacher was keen to find out if the printed image looked the way the child had expected it to look. There were some inconsistencies in the colours which (with the teacher guidance) the child noticed. The teacher then talked to him about how he could achieve a darker red next time. The focus of the questioning was on the work the printer had produced. This is a subtle point; here the teacher is introducing the notion of reviewing and reflecting on work but focusing it on the printer not the child. In effect 'How can you develop and improve your work?' has become, 'What can we do to make sure the printer prints the way you want it to?' There is no implied criticism of the child's work.

Reflective task

Think of the types of questions and intervention strategies you could employ with very young children to make them more aware of the work they have produced.

How can you do this carefully so that the child considers their work, but without appearing to criticise or demean their efforts?

The learning intention in the above example was *to use 'click and drag' to move icons into selected positions*, and much of the discussion revolved around this. However, the discussion (led by the teacher) developed into a comparison between the screen image and the printed one and an encouragement of the children's comments regarding how this affected their completed work. Questions regarding how the work could be improved allowed he children to propose modifications to their work. However, the knowledge and understanding associated with revising and modifying work need not have specific learning intention. Developing the children's skills of self awareness and critical reflection of their own work should be seen as part of almost every session.

Reflective task

Think of some of the taught sessions you have had in the past.

When working with children, interacting and discussing their work, were there any opportunities to help them to develop their skills of self-reflection?

How could you plan for such opportunities for the future?

Key Stage I

'Developing, evaluating and refining' is not purely an individual activity. A great deal of learning is founded on co-operatively achieved success. Children can often learn and achieve more with others than they can on their own. It has been argued that one of the reasons why humans are the most successful animal species on the planet is because we are *able to combine the flexibility and experimental brilliance of individuals with the generative power of co-operative effort* (Fisher, 1995, p90).

It is essential, then, that there are times when children are offered opportunities to work in pairs or groups. Indeed, when working with ICT, the collaborative approach offers a great deal of benefits. However, for this to work effectively children need to be comfortable working together. Unfortunately, their ability to collaborate is sometimes hampered because their listening and communicating skills are not sophisticated enough. As Dawes, Mercer and Wegerif have pointed out:

> the quality of children's work with computers can be greatly improved if they are taught how to talk and listen to each other face to face. Technology can provide new opportunities but the essential skill of communication lies in knowing how to reach a shared understanding (2000, p62)

The following is an example of where a teacher designed a series of teaching and learning sessions specifically so that the pupils could work in pairs to share design ideas and evaluate them together. The pupils were working with a 3D design program Spex+ Environment Designer. This program allows children to quickly design 'environments' such as classrooms, shops, gardens, streets and even Egyptian tombs. In the following example the pupils were working with a bedroom 'environment' (see Figure 8.1). They could use specific 2D and 3D images of household furniture and place these in the room. A number of features can be adjusted, such as the size of the room, furniture styles, and the colours of the walls. Any of the elements (furniture, etc) can be changed easily and there is a large range to choose from. The teacher made good use of this in the following activity.

Teaching example 8.3

Year 2
ICT learning intention: to work collaboratively to use a graphical modelling program to explore alternative design ideas.

Design technology learning intention: to use their own experience to generate new ideas to satisfy specific criteria.

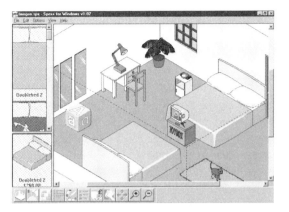

Figure 8.1. Spex+ image

The teacher asked the children to to think about their bedroom in their house. They were encouraged to create a list of typical items they would find in their room. The children then worked in pairs, to collaboratively produce an idea of what constitutes an 'ideal bedroom'.

The teacher then demonstrated elements of the Spex+ program. She showed how to select different items of furniture and then place them in the room. Next she asked the children to begin designing their own room using the Spex+ program. As the children worked together they learned that they were able change the layout of the furniture, thus learning they could modify and adapt the room with the help of the program. The children saved and then printed out their work. As a class the children then discussed each room layout and suggested how, if necessary, the layouts could be improved.

In a subsequent lesson, once children had gained some experience and were confident using the program's tools to design and remodel rooms, the teacher told the children they were going to design a room for a specific family. She gave each group of children a different scenario card. This was a card with a short description of a family's needs written on it. The information made it clear what type of room the family needed and the things they would like to find there, for example:

The Jones family need a bedroom for their daughter, Julie.

Julie is five years old. Her favourite colour is pink. She likes horses and would love a bedroom with lots of room to play and a big old-fashioned bed.

The children were challenged to think about the family's needs and create a room that suited them.

At the end of the task the children came together to share their printed rooms and scenario cards. The teacher questioned them and encouraged them to question each other regarding their decisions for different choices made for the rooms.

Remember that reviewing and modifying will not happen alone. Planning should ensure that there is sufficient time at the end of each session for the children to reflect on, evaluate and modify their work.

When the children are engaged in reviewing their work the skills they will be developing are not dissimilar to the evaluation skills student (and qualified) teachers are constantly developing when considering their own practice. Consequently, many of the evaluation and self-review practices can be undertaken with the children and their own work, in particular the following.

- **Evaluation should not wait until the end of the session. Children should be encouraged to evaluate as they proceed with their work.**
- **Children should be encouraged to ask themselves 'What have I learnt? How would I improve my work? Where do I need to go next?'**
- **The value of evaluation comes when the children are able to state how closely their work/product matches what was intended.**
- **Evaluation of the work should lead the children to begin to evaluate the 'processes' they worked through.**
- **Children need to develop the skills of being able to look objectively at their work. All the work they produce and every idea they have cannot be consistently poor, or consistently 'perfect'.**
- **As children gain experience, they also need to be open to the thoughts and evaluations of others, seeing these thoughts not as personal criticisms but as constructive learning points.**

Key Stage 2

At Key Stage 2 children will be using a broader range of ICT applications and skills. Their reviewing, modifying and evaluation work may well include the use of numerical data in spreadsheets and databases. For instance, the Teaching example 2.6, in Chapter 2, detailed the use of a spreadsheet as part of a number investigation. Here, the nature of provisionality allowed the children to experiment with a range of different numbers. Working together they were able to collaborate within the problem-solving and refine their skills. The ICT removed the burden of repetitive calculation and the children were able to quickly and easily refine and modify their ideas as they worked with the spreadsheet.

These concepts can similarly be applied to written work, as the following example illustrates.

Teaching example 8.4

Year 4
ICT learning intention: to develop and refine ideas by creating and reorganising text.

Literacy learning intention: to use alliteration as the structure for a poem.

The children had been working on a number of alliteration poems. Rather than doing this as a paper and pencil exercise the teacher planned that they would

work in groups using ICT. The children worked together to generate some ideas for line beginnings, they entered the beginnings of the lines and then experimented with different words, adjusting and editing as they went. Some of the children used the word processor's thesaurus facility to broaden their word choice. They then experimented with different line endings and when they were satisfied they saved and printed their work. Once they saw the printout, some children felt that the font and text size did not suit the paper properly so decided to adjust the size of the font and reformat the title. They reloaded their writing, edited it and printed it once more.

Word processing is most effective when used with first and second drafts, but children will not appreciate or use this facility if the act of revision is not actually taught. In the example above, the teacher encouraged the children to use the word processor screen almost as a note pad to test, to try and to experiment with different words and phrases. This form of generating and amending text is a more purposeful use of word processing software than the notion of typing up a neat version from notes written in a work book. This exercise helps to free creativity and improve collaboration, the typing-up exercise serves only to demote ICT and turn it into a tool for presenting and publishing work. Presenting 'neat work' is a fine use for ICT, but it is only one small feature of word processing or publishing software. To use ICT well, children need to be given opportunities to experience a more complete range of tools, such as cutting and pasting text, using dictionary and thesaurus tools and making use of automatic correction facilities.

The reviewing functions in Microsoft Word are also useful, professional, features which children can employ. For example, using the 'insert comment' function will allow children to note down extra thoughts, ideas or questions as they occur to them during their writing. The insert comment feature is most useful for collaborative work since children can leave comments, or notes, within the text, suggesting improvements or modifications. Also, the teacher can employ the insert comment feature to offer focused feedback to the children about their work.

When working in an ICT suite, the comment tool can be useful as a management tool for the teacher. The teacher can encourage the children to add a note to their work if they are uncertain about anything. Then, when the teacher is next working with that group they can discuss and address any problems together.

Like other ICT techniques discussed earlier, word processing is most effective and productive when it is the result of collaborative work. It is important when grouping children for collaborative work that the dynamics of the group are considered.

Reflective task

When grouping (or pairing) children for ICT work consider the following questions.

- *Why are you grouping them?*
- *Do the children have the necessary communication and social skills to work together?*

- Are you using mixed ability? If so, are you mixing them according to their ICT skills or their strengths in another curriculum area?
- Have the children been assigned roles in their 'team'?
- Are the children clear about their roles?
- Are the children expected to change roles during the task?
- Are the children clear about the purpose of the task?

A starting point for reviewing, modifying and evaluating written work can be to give the children a piece of text that already contains errors, and asking the children to correct and improve it. If the original text is presented as a word processing file then the children can make full use of ICT tools to find errors and modify the work. For example, the children can be given a:

- piece of instructional text with the instructions in the wrong order;
- short paragraph with a number of spelling errors;
- piece of text containing mixed tenses;
- number of short paragraphs containing several disorganised ideas; the children have to re-work the text to improve the sense;
- piece of text written for an adult which the children have to adapt so that it is understandable by a five year old;
- story about an old wizard that the children have to change to a story about a young princess;
- letter of praise which the children have to transform into a letter of complaint.

For most of these activities the children will be developing their use of cut and paste, or search and replace tools. These kinds of tasks have a clear focus on literacy and are related to the tasks discussed in Part 3 (Textual Communication). However, the contexts in which these tasks are planned can be as diverse as history, geography, religious education or science. For example a class working on a project on Henry VIII could be presented with an 'email' that was sent to Henry describing the events surrounding the sinking of the *Mary Rose*, but with many of the elements in the wrong order, or poorly phrased. The children's task, using their historical knowledge and ICT skills of reviewing, modifying and evaluating, would be to correct and improve the text.

The essential feature is that the tasks have a tight focus on ICT skills, specifically: the development of reviewing, modifying and evaluating skills.

Practical task

Consider the tasks described above. Can you plan an alternative literacy activity which offers the same tight ICT focus?

When you are next planning a literacy session, note two or three examples of when the literacy strategy requires pupils to undertake detailed written work. Can you develop these so that the pupils will have an opportunity to use ICT and, if appropriate, the 'insert comment' tool?

In order to develop pupils' knowledge, understanding and skills of reviewing, modifying and evaluating it is important to give them:

- plenty of opportunity to practise and to solve problems more than once;
- regular feedback on how they are getting on;
- opportunities to review what went well and think about what they will do next time;
- encouragement to evaluate their work and, if necessary, to record their thoughts;
- an opportunity to see others' work and to talk to them about their approaches and solutions.

Practical task

When grouping the pupils for an ICT activity consider the following.

What is the task the group will be working on?
Is the ICT appropriate for a group?
Why are the children being grouped?

The following example is a development of a design technology focused lesson from Key Stage I (Teaching example 8.3).

Teaching example 8.5

Year 5

ICT learning intention: to work with others to explore a variety of alternative designs using a graphical modelling program.

Mathematics learning intention: to use addition and subtraction to solve real life problems.

As part of a project on advertising the pupils were considering the design of a shop. The children had been collecting information about local businesses. The teacher explained that they were going to use a computer program to help them design and create a shop. She then demonstrated the 'shop' environment of the Spex+ design program. The children were familiar with most of the facilities of the program from work they had undertaken in a previous class. The teacher had planned to extend their knowledge and skills by involving them in using the program's budgeting feature.

Working in pairs, the children were asked to design a shop using some of the furniture and fittings available within the Spex+ program. While the children were choosing their fittings and starting to plan their shop, the teacher explained that they had to work to a budget. By using the program's spreadsheet facility the teacher demonstrated the implications of choosing different types of shop fittings. Expensive shop units, for example, deducted large amounts from the budget. The children could see how much they were

---

spending on each item, and could use this information to help them make decisions about their design. The teacher had to encourage some children to rethink their designs when they found they had overspent.

The focus for the remainder of the session was on directing the children to think about how a budget may restrict choices, and how they may have to change their design a number of times before all of the factors (aesthetic and financial) are satisfied.

Reflective task

Teaching example 8.5 built directly on children's prior experience of working with the same program in Key Stage 1.

When working on an ICT project such as this how can you be sure what prior knowledge the children have had of the software?

Is the fact that children have had an opportunity to use the software enough, or do you need to know about their specific capabilities and level of confidence? How can you determine this information?

This chapter has illustrated a number of practical ways of supporting children while they are developing their ICT skills. The focus has been on developing their skills to review, modify and evaluate their work. Clearly, the knowledge, understanding and skills should be emphasised and encouraged throughout all work and across all curriculum areas.

Practical task

Consider the following strategies for supporting pupils with their developing ICT skills. Make a note of those you feel you might use in your future teaching.

When pupils are working in pairs, when would you:

- *Assign a specific role to each pupil?*
- *Set a different task or target for each pupil?*
- *Use a timer so pupils can swap roles?*
- *Arrange the pairing so that a pupil with less confidence with ICT is supported by one with good ICT capabilities?*

In your teaching, when would you:

- *Demonstrate a technique to a small group who then demonstrate this to other groups?*
- *Plan a common project but offer different targets to different groups?*
- *Allow pupils to choose their own tasks?*
- *Give specific groups different amounts of time to complete a set task?*
- *Provide a series of tasks increasing in difficulty so that pupils can work at their own pace?*

Reviewing, modifying and evaluating in practice:
a summary of key points

There are several important features when considering the development of pupils' reviewing, modifying and evaluating skills. These skills:

— *are greatly enhanced by ICT programs that permit pupils to refine or amend their work easily (provisionality);*

— *can best be addressed and developed through cross-curricular work;*

— *are closely linked to pupils' development and effective use of speaking and listening;*

— *develop most effectively where pupils are involved in collaborative work.*

References

Costello, P. J. M. (2003) *Thinking skills and early childhood education*. London: David Fulton

Dawes, L., Mercer, N. and Wegerif, R., (2000) *Extending talk and reasoning skills in Teaching and learning with ICT in the primary school*, Leask, M. and Meadows, J. (eds) London: Routledge.

Fisher, R. (1995) *Teaching children to learn*. Cheltenham: Stanley Thornes.

Kenny, J. (2000) *Times Educational Supplement*: English Curriculum special feature. London: TES.

QCA (2000) *Curriculum guidance for the Foundation Stage*. London: QCA.

Further reading

Costello, P. J. M. (2003) *Thinking skills and early childhood education*. London: David Fulton. Costello discusses the nature and purpose of a 'thinking' curriculum, and provides clear evidence that the teaching of thinking skills has much to offer the curriculum of infant, primary and secondary schools.

Resources

Spark Island Farmer Rumtums Letter Fun 3-5 published jointly by Spark Island and the BBC. Further details from www.sparkisland.com.

Kid Pix published by Research Machines. Further details from www.rm.com/primary.

Spex+ Environment Designer published by Aspex Software. Further details from www.aspexsoftware.com.

9 ICT STRATEGIES: REVIEWING, MODIFYING AND EVALUATING

By the end of this chapter you should:

- be aware of where 'reviewing, modifying and evaluating' fits within the curriculum;
- be aware of the starting points for reviewing, modifying and evaluating;
- understand the importance of collaborative work for developing reviewing, modifying and evaluating skills;
- be able to plan and organise learning in creative ways to enable children to access activities where reviewing, modifying and evaluating will be purposeful;
- be able to suggest ways of differentiating ICT activities which involve reviewing, modifying and evaluating;
- be aware of possible ways of assessing children's ICT capability;
- recognise the importance of involving children in their own assessment;
- recognise the importance of reflecting on your own practice to identify areas of strength and those in need of development.

Professional Standards for QTS
Q2.1, Q2.2, Q2.3, Q2.6, Q2.7, Q3.2, Q3.3, Q3.4, Q3.5

Links to the Foundation Stage Guidance and the National Curriculum

In the Foundation Stage children will use information communication technology to support their learning.

At Key Stage I children will review what they have done to help them develop their ideas, describe the effects of their actions and talk about what they might change in future work (4a, 4b, 4c). Children will also work with a range of information to investigate the different ways it can be presented, explore a variety of ICT tools and talk about the uses of ICT outside and inside school (5a, 5b, 5c).

At Key Stage 2 children will review what they and others have done to help them develop their ideas, describe and talk about the effectiveness of their work with ICT, comparing it with other methods and considering the effect it has on others (4a, 4b), and talk about how they could improve future work. Throughout their work, children should work with others to explore a variety of information sources, and be involved in investigating and comparing the uses of ICT inside and outside school.

Introduction

What the National Curriculum for ICT describes as 'Reviewing, Modifying and Evaluating Work as it Progresses' (from here referred to as RME) is an interesting aspect of learning. Clearly, the notions of reflection, assessment and improvement are central themes of learning. This development of self-knowledge crosses all areas of ICT, and encompasses all subject areas. It is treated here as a separate unit only for ease of discussion. It is easy to think of RME taking place within a literacy session. Here pupils, using a word processor, evaluate and adapt words, sentences or whole passages of text. However, pupils will also be involved in using RME skills when they consider their developing abilities in art, or their growing understanding of historical or geographical issues. ICT has a major part to play across all subject areas. Video imaging, for example, can help to determine exactly what went well with a particular PE movement; the association of images and text on screen can help children to determine the effectiveness of a scientific presentation.

As was discussed in Chapter 8, the ease with which ICT work can be adapted makes it a powerful tool for assisting with the development of, and easing children into, using RME strategies. However, if children do not feel comfortable evaluating or modifying their work, then even with the support of well planned ICT activities, they will find the process demotivating. Consequently, there are a number of important factors to be considered when encouraging RME, these are:

- **the learning climate and self-esteem;**
- **the teacher's role;**
- **the relevance of the activity;**
- **the place of collaborative work;**
- **self-assessment.**

These will be considered in detail throughout this chapter.

Tools and strategies

The learning climate and self-esteem

A positive learning climate is essential when pupils are dealing with the development of RME skills. Pupils will be engaged in commenting openly on their work and the work of others. This could be seen as personal criticism; consequently some pupils may feel threatened. This will be reduced if the ethos of the classroom is one of consideration and sharing. It should be clear to the pupils that everyone's view is important and that changes and improvements are acceptable. ICT supports this notion, since material can be edited and re-edited as many times as necessary. If the pupils decide that their initial idea could be improved, or if they identify a mistake, they should be encouraged to use this as a positive step. Otherwise, if a pupil has a distinct fear of failure it will restrict them from attempting a different route, or trying a novel approach. Occasionally, the fear of failure can cause some pupils to lose motivation if they do not 'get it right', or to deliberately destroy their own work.

If the main focus is on pupils' limitations they will spend the majority of the session working thorough their weak areas, and focusing on what they do badly. This will lower their self-esteem, and consequently affect their interest and motivation.

In order to develop the most effective learning climate it is important to build on the children's strengths by giving them opportunities to use their talents to achieve success. Teaching example 8.5 illustrated an activity where children revisited a computer design program they had used in an earlier year. Their familiarity with its tools and their skills with using them effectively enabled them to concentrate on developing their use more fully. However, in a greater sense, the children had a shared understanding of what could be done and how they could achieve it.

In order to preserve pupils' self-confidence and self-esteem, there needs to be a good balance between feedback which offers suggestions for improvement, and feedback which celebrates successes. For some pupils (and adults), self-evaluatory work is often difficult in the beginning. Some children want to offer a consistently high evaluation of their work, others tend to be too self-critical (as was discussed on page 106). The ability to realistically evaluate one's own performance improves with practice and is both empowering and highly motivating.

The teacher's role

As a teacher you can provide direct support to pupils as they work on RME skills. Some may need reassurance that the decisions they are making are effective. Others may need to develop specific skills to help them become more aware of the need for reviewing or modifying. These elements will be discussed later. However, a further important issue is your role in modelling RME approaches.

As a role model, you can demonstrate being an effective learner, a calm, organised person, a good loser, etc. It is important to model the processes of RME on all occasions. Whenever a flaw or error is noticed, model the process of questioning, reflecting and then modifying the mistake. As you have no doubt experienced, if you have ever made an error in a lesson, children are quick to tell you where you have gone wrong. It is important to use these opportunities to illustrate the RME process.

Other opportunities to model RME skills and processes should be planned as a specific part of your teaching. For example, when demonstrating a painting program it is important to demonstrate how to 'undo' effects and operations that go badly. It is also useful to encourage the children to take part in this – starting a simple picture, asking for their opinion, making adjustments, asking the pupils to judge the effectiveness of the result, and making changes in light of this.

With collaborative writing, the use of a white board will enable you to quickly adjust the content in the light of your (and their) ongoing evaluations of the work. It is important to stress that this is a good thing to do, and that the changes will improve the work.

When working with musical composition software, model the RME process as the composition is being developed. Demonstrate the workings of the program and enlist the pupils in suggesting a series of phrases. Make some deliberate mistakes and rectify them calmly and efficiently. Discuss the musical sequence at intervals and encourage the children to identify what they like about it, and how it can be improved.

All these examples enable the teacher to model elements of the Key Stage I requirements: children should *review what they have done to help them develop their ideas* (4a) and *talk about what they might change in future work* (4c).

These opportunities can be effectively planned as part of the introductory section of teaching sessions. However, it is important to maintain the modelling process during the main part of sessions and to return to it as part of the plenary.

Practical task

For your next ICT teaching session think carefully about the plenary. What questions can you ask to promote the following.

- *Encouraging pupils to think about the processes they have gone through to produce their work?*
- *Enabling pupils to consider, and to share, their experiences of reviewing, modifying and evaluating?*

The relevance of the activity

The work the children undertake has to be purposeful, have meaning for them and be relevant to their needs.

Short, tightly focused activities are most effective for developing ICT skills. Teaching example 8.1, in Chapter 8, illustrated an activity in which the pupils selected and moved screen icons. The ICT skills were focused on 'mouse control'. The context was literacy, recognition of phonemes in C-V-C words. The pupils spent only a short period of time using the software. In this time they practised mouse control repeatedly and developed that skill alongside the reinforcement that the program gave to their understanding of C-V-C words.

Longer, open-ended activities will help pupils to develop a broader range of skills. Teaching example 8.2 described the use of a painting program. The ICT learning intention was similar to the previous activity: 'click and drag' mouse control. The context was creativity development. The pupils were highly motivated to develop their repeated pattern and, again, practised their mouse skills. The activity was more open-ended. Where the first example had a single answer (children had to select the correct phoneme to complete the C-V-C word), this one had no 'right' answer (children were creating a pattern with a repeat). Consequently, the pupils were expected to remain at the task for longer, the ICT skills they developed were broader and they had a longer time to practise them. The creative freedom within the task and the fact that they could stop, erase the pattern and start again at any time helped to maintain their motivation and interest. At the end of the activity the teacher engaged the pupils in a discussion regarding the effectiveness of the painting program and then (gently) led them to consider how they might change the pattern if they had a chance to do it again.

This is not to suggest that open-ended activities are automatically more purposeful than focused ones. Both the above examples were successful on their own terms. Your decision on which to use will depend upon the pupils' abilities and needs, the nature of the task and the learning intentions you plan to cater for.

Those learning intentions are of prime importance for you (your planning) and for the pupils. Older pupils who do not automatically understand the significance of an activity will be unenthusiastic. However, establishing and sharing the learning intentions, and the success criteria, with them will enable them to understand the reasons for the task.

When encouraging pupils to take on greater challenges with ICT it is important to provide the structure and guidance to make their work and their learning successful. Therefore, it may be necessary to scaffold some activities. You, as the teacher, may need to offer greater support, or adapt an activity to meet the needs of specific pupils. It is important to remember that if a pupil is easily succeeding with a task then he/she is merely practising something they are familiar with.

The place of collaborative work

It is important to realise that there is a distinction between group work and collaborative work. Group work can be seen more as a management tool, whereas collaborative work is more a 'process'. It is perfectly feasible to have children working as a group but having little collaboration; similarly, children can collaborate on work without actually working side by side (see Table 9.1).

Table 9.1. Group work and collaboration

Group work involves	Collaboration involves
• *initiating an activity;* • *seeking information and opinions;* • *giving information and opinions;* • *elaborating on ideas and concepts;* • *co-ordinating a group's activity;* • *summarising the learning outcomes.*	• *encouraging each other;* • *allowing others to speak;* • *setting standards;* • *accepting others' opinions and decisions;* • *expressing 'group' feelings.*

(Adapted from Bennett and Dunne, 1992)

Technological developments are changing the notion of 'group work' in that it is perfectly possible for children to collaborate on a piece of text without actually seeing each other. Some of this can be synchronous, where all parties working on the text have access at the same time. Working over a network, for example, children can communicate and adjust information in a spreadsheet or a word processed document, the work being opened on multiple machines at the same time. Pupils can also be involved in editing and working on projects non-synchronously, where each accesses the text at different times. For example, as part of a writing project, pupils can email a story to another school where their collaborator reviews, adapts and adds to the text before returning it. Similarly, pupils can collaborate with others in the class by saving a document for another pupil to open and edit. Modifications and comments can be recorded (in MS Word, for example) with the use of 'comment' markers, or by working in text of a different colour. When children are collaborating with others in situations where they cannot see them directly, the lines of communication and agreement have to be clear.

For collaborative work to be successful, pupils must develop the necessary skills. Firstly, children need to be able to co-operate. They need to *have a developing awareness of their own needs, views and feelings and be sensitive to the needs, views and feelings of others* (QCA, 2000, p34). This may need to be developed as a specific skill, particularly in the early years. Young children need activities where they can practise:

- **taking part;**
- **taking turns;**
- **listening to others;**
- **questioning others;**
- **helping others;**
- **offering praise and encouragement.**

This can be encouraged through the use of small group games and play activities. In the Foundation Stage this may be board games, 'show and tell' times, responsibilities, circle time activities. These are all areas which overlap into personal, social and emotional development, as well as communication, language and literacy.

There are obvious links between the development of collaborative work and of speaking and listening skills. Pupils will need plenty of opportunities to talk purposefully, listen, respond, ask questions and co-operate in different groups.

Reflective task

If it is appropriate for your pupils in your next school, make a class list of the speaking and listening skills and ask them to think about which skills they have developed well, and which ones they need to work on.

The skills of effective, purposeful discussion also need to be identified and taught. Specific ICT programs can help develop these areas: Kar2ouch, Developing Tray, and concept mapping programs such as 2connect, for example. Pupils should also be encouraged to take some responsibility for their learning by involving them in making decisions and through the use of self-evaluation.

Practical task

Discussion is a useful tool for involving children in the learning process. However, without meaningful, significant intervention from an adult, the amount of learning taking place is difficult to quantify. Some children will lack the skills with which to develop and explore an issue in depth.

Plan ways in which you can support children with their discussion work.

As children move through the primary phase their co-operative skills should be developed to include:

- interviewing and questioning each other;
- empathetic listening;
- describing accurately;
- editing and summarising information;
- negotiating a common agreement;
- supporting others to achieve a successful outcome.

Computers are very powerful facilitators of group work. Many of the applications present challenges which stimulate children to discuss and to share. Teaching examples in Chapter 8 illustrated activities in which pupils were paired in order for them to discuss the important features of a bedroom (Teaching example 8.3) and the selection of words for an alliterative poem (Teaching example 8.4). The provisional features of the two programs meant that the pupils could discuss, share, adapt, refine, review, modify... until they were happy with the choices they had made. The latter (word processing) activity illustrated the effectiveness of pupils working collaboratively and redrafting work. The teacher had paired the pupils for this task and they worked closely together, this is sometimes called a 'buddy system' or 'response partners'. This is when pairs of children work closely together; to support and assess each other with an activity. This is the form of peer assessment which Black et al. described as being valuable because students often give and receive criticism of their work more freely than in the traditional teacher/student interchange (Black et al., 2003). If peer relationships are not good, however, there can be some difficulties with this approach, and these will be discussed later. The Black report identified a further support for this form of assessment, however. That is the nature of the language which children use when assessing: the language used by students to each other is the language they would naturally use, rather than 'school' language (Black et al., 2003).

Reflective task

Look at some of the online activities below. Decide how you could use them to develop collaborative work. Make a note of what questioning techniques or interventions you would need to use to help the children gain the most from them.

General activities: www.mape.org.uk/activities/index.htm.
General white board resources: www.bgfl.org.bgfl/15.cfm.
History: www.learningcurve.gov.uk/index/.

Self-assessment

In order to fully implement RME in all their work pupils need to be fully aware of what it is they are aiming to achieve. If they are using music software and are asked to combine a series of musical icons to produce a tune, how will they know when they have achieved that? In order to effectively review their work they need to know what the outcome should be. It is helpful to share the learning intentions with the pupils so they are aware of the purpose and context of the work. However, for some activities, these are not specific enough for the children to judge how effective their work has been. In these cases it is useful to identify 'success criteria' which the children can use to help them determine how effective their work has been. In Teaching example 8.3 the learning intentions were:

ICT learning intention: to work collaboratively to use a graphical modelling program to explore alternative design ideas.

Design and technology learning intention: to use their own experience to generate new ideas to satisfy specific criteria.

The activity involved generating a suitable bedroom design for a specific person, and this would be the focus of the success criteria.

In some cases it will be useful for the pupils themselves to identify their own success criteria before they begin the activity.

Practical task

Look back at your planning for a recent school experience. Find an ICT session and revisit the learning intentions and the activity you devised for that session.

• **Did you promote elements of RME in your planning?**

Make a note of the success criteria that would have been appropriate for that activity.

• **Were there opportunities for some pupils to devise their own success criteria?**
• **What strategies could you use to enable the pupils to know how effective they were at meeting the success criteria?**

Many teachers formalise the use of pupils' self-assessment by asking specific questions of the children during the main part of the session, or as part of the plenary. The pupils are encouraged to quickly share their views regarding their assessment of their work in several ways.

Some teachers ask the children to show a 'thumbs up/thumbs down' gesture depending upon their feelings regarding their work. An alternative is a 'show me five' request. The teacher asks how effectively the children feel they have accomplished the task, or if they feel they have met the success criteria. The children respond by holding up a hand to show one or more fingers. The more fingers they show the more confidence they have in their work.

It is also important to formalise this process, and many schools use assessment task sheets. These can help pupils to further focus on their development of RME. The self-assessment records tend to focus on three areas: what the children like about their work, how they improved it and what they feel they need to do next time they work on a similar activity (see Figure 9.1).

I am happy with this piece of work because...
I have improved it by...
Next time I need to...

Figure 9.1. Self-assessment task sheet

These self-assessment techniques all help children to become more aware of their own capabilities and encourage them to develop RME skills. However, an important element of RME is that pupils should be considering the effectiveness of their work and the development of their skills as the work progresses, not just at the end of the session. It is therefore important to consider strategies to help pupils to focus on this throughout the session, either by stopping the work at intervals and asking questions of the whole group, or by intervening with individual children.

One such strategy for engaging pupils in self-assessment could be to give them a sticky note on which to draw a smiley face. A clear smile indicates full understanding, contentment with the task and good progress being made; a frown indicates less contentment and a sad face would suggest that the child was struggling with a problem. The children attach the sticky notes to the top edge of their computer monitor so the teacher can quickly assess where additional support may be needed. Pupils seem to find this a very unthreatening way of asking for support; sticky notes are, by their very nature, non-permanent and this lends a transitory feeling to the action of asking for help. As a management strategy, the notes are also especially useful when you are working with groups in a computer suite.

Professional issues

The use of RME is important for professional purposes. All teachers are constantly involved in self-evaluations of their work and practices. As a student teacher you will be expected to evaluate your session organisation, your planning and delivery. Evaluation is a skill, and you will be required to reflect upon and evaluate your work. This reflection might be through discussions with the class teacher, or your mentor, and it may be informal or formal in nature. The evaluations could also be part of a written record of your development. Any evaluation or reflection you do should add value to the learning you are undertaking. You will need to be both objective and self-critical of the work and its results in order to see the benefits.

Practical task

Think carefully about how you proceed with the task of evaluating your work.

- *How clear are you about the elements that you do well? How well do you recognise the areas where you need to develop?*
- *What evidence is there to suggest that you are doing well?*
- *Can you use your strategies and feelings here to help when explaining the RME processes to the pupils?*

In the process of undertaking self-evaluation tasks yourself, you will have a good insight into the feelings the pupils will have when they undertake the same process. When children are involved in collaborating on RME tasks they are effectively peer-assessing their work. This can have quite a different emotional impact. Imagine your student friends watching you and then sharing their thoughts. It is highly likely that you would welcome this from some friends, but resist the idea with other individuals. The same is going to be true with young children. Therefore it is essential to have some agreed rules when children are paired as response partners or 'buddies'.

The Primary National Strategy Professional Development Materials identify the following useful strategies.

- **Both partners should be of roughly the same ability, or just one jump ahead or behind, rather than a wide gap.**
- **The pupils need time to reflect on and check their own work or ideas before their response partner offers suggestions.**
- **The response partner should always begin with a sincere, positive comment.**
- **The roles of the partners need to be clearly identified.**
- **The response partner needs time to consider the ideas presented and time to consider suggestions. If the work is written it is helpful if the author reads the work out first; this establishes ownership of the piece.**
- **If it is suggested that an element should be modified, then both pupils must agree before the change is made.**
- **The author should make the marks on the work as a result of the paired discussion.**
- **Pupils need to be reminded that the focus of the task is the learning intention.**
- **The response partner should ask for clarification before jumping to conclusions.**
- **The improvement suggestions should be verbal and not written down. The only writing necessary should be the successes and the improvement itself.**
- **It would be useful to role play response partners in front of the class. Possibly showing them the wrong way and the right way over a piece of work.**

- It could be useful to do this two-thirds of the way through the lesson – so the children can make an improvement and continue writing with a better understanding of quality.

(Adapted from DfES, 2004)

Organisation and differentiation

It has been suggested a number of times that ICT is most effective as a collaborative exercise. Even within resource-rich environments where children have the opportunity to work individually on computers or with other ICT equipment, it is still desirable to arrange for them to work in pairs for some tasks. However, when pupils work together, there are many factors that can affect the quality of their collaborative learning. Their confidence in their own skills, their interpersonal relationships, and occasionally gender issues will affect the openness with which they approach the activity.

When organising children in the class to work on ICT projects it may be useful to consider some of the following grouping strategies.

Paired work where:

- individuals are set specifically defined tasks;
- pupils have individually defined success criteria;
- pairs swap roles after a defined period of time.

Sessions where you:

- demonstrate an ICT skill to a group who then plan and demonstrate this to small groups;
- plan a project but provide different starting points and set different targets;
- enable the pupils to choose from a restricted range of activities which meet the same learning intention;
- provide a series of staged activities where pupils are guided to select their own starting point;
- allow pupils to determine the order in which they work through a set of activities;
- set different time-scales for pupils with differing levels of skill;
- give pupils working on a task specific roles to play.

Practical task

From the above strategies identify those that you feel would be useful for you in your next school experience.

Think of other organisational strategies, ask your class teacher or your mentor what strategies they use, so you can add to the above list.

As the teacher you will need to be very aware of all the social dynamics within the class when organising the groups. At times it may be useful to allow the children to choose their own partners based on their friendships. At other times you may feel the learning intentions and the needs of the activity will be served better if the pupils are paired according to ability. Occasionally you may need to organise the children so that a pupil lacking in confidence can be supported by one with greater ICT capabilities. Your knowledge of the children, their needs and what you want them to learn will be paramount in deciding on the groupings.

Reviewing, modifying and evaluating work:
a summary of key points

- **Pupils' opportunities to use RME skills are greatly enhanced by ICT programs that permit them to refine or amend their work easily (provisionality).**
- **RME is closely associated with the skills of reflection and self-evaluation.**
- **It is crucial for pupils' self-esteem that the learning climate is conducive to self-questioning and reflection.**
- **RME skills are closely linked to pupils' development and effective use of speaking and listening.**
- **RME develops most effectively where pupils are involved in collaborative work.**

References

Bennett, N. and Dunne, E. (1992) *Managing classroom groups*. Hemel Hempstead: Simon & Schuster Education.

Black, P., Harrison, C., Lee, C., Marshall, B. and Wiliam, D. (2003) *Working inside the black box: assessment for learning in the classroom*. London: King's College.

Call, N. (2003) *The thinking child: brain-based learning for the foundation stage*. Stafford: Network Educational Press.

DfES (2004) *Primary National Strategy professional development materials: assessment for learning*. London: DfES.

QCA (2000) *Curriculum guidance for the Foundation Stage*. London: QCA.

Further reading

Black, P., Harrison, C., Lee, C., Marshall, B. and Wiliam, D. (2003) *Assessment for Learning: Putting it into practice*. London: OUP. The authors use their research and personal experience to fully explain how formative assessment can improve pupils' learning They also carefully detail a series of case studies to demonstrate how 'Assessment for Learning' can be managed in the classroom.

Resources

QCA Teacher's Guide for Information and Communication Technology.
Exemplifies integrated tasks from this QCA guide. Available from: www.standards. dfes.gov.uk/schemes.

10 CONTROL TECHNOLOGY IN PRACTICE

By the end of this chapter you should:

- *identify what control technology is and its associated devices;*
- *have an understanding of the broad nature of control technology;*
- *be aware of the ways in which control technology can be used in the classroom;*
- *have an understanding of the skills progression within control technology;*
- *appreciate the range of ways in which ICT can support subject learning.*

Professional Standards for QTS
Q2.1, Q2.2, Q2.4, Q2.6, Q3.3

Links to the Foundation Stage Guidance and the National Curriculum

In the Foundation Stage children will use information communication technology to support their learning.

At Key Stage 1 children will plan and give instructions to make things happen, try things out and explore what happens in real and imaginary situations (2c, 2d).

At Key Stage 2 children will create, test, improve and refine sequences of instructions to make things happen and to monitor events and respond to them. They will also use simulations and explore models in order to answer 'what if?' type questions, to investigate and evaluate the effect of changing values and to identify patterns and relationships (2b, 2c).

Introduction

Control technology is an unusual area of the curriculum. We all use control technology every day, often without even realising it. Although children use control technology regularly, opportunities to actually develop and explore their skills in the classroom can be limited. This is highlighted by the fact that control technology is still identified as one of the most challenging areas for schools. The QCA 2004/5 annual report for ICT indicates that 'the teaching and assessment of data logging and control are still of concern in over half of schools' (QCA, 2005, p11).

When children use the television remote control, play with a programmable toy or programme the video they are using control technology. Control systems are in use in almost every 'everyday' appliance from automatic kettles, alarm clocks, central heating systems, DVD players to alarms in shops when you have picked up a radio that you want to look at. Because of this familiarity, it is relatively easy for children to understand how and why control technology is beneficial.

Control involves causing something to happen by giving an instruction. For example, a light comes on when you switch on a torch. A simple procedure therefore can cause an event to occur.

The Foundation Stage Curriculum Guidance suggests that children need to develop an awareness of the ways in which ICT can help us. Clearly, control technology has a strong link here and it is not difficult to encourage the children to discuss and describe the types of technology they have had experience with and to discuss the ways technology can help to control events or objects.

Throughout Key Stages I and 2, the National Curriculum programme of study indicates that children should be involved, controlling technology by using instructions. One of the clearest ways of doing this is through the use of programmable toys or floor robots. These will be discussed in detail later in the chapter and in Chapter II.

In Key Stage 2 children should be involved in testing, improving and refining sequences of instructions to make things happen. Again, floor robots offer a unique starting point for this, but children can also use specific control unit equipment. A control unit is usually connected to a computer. It has a number of sockets for connecting devices to it (alarms, motors, lights.) The control unit acts as a switch that controls any devices connected to it. Some control units also have sockets for sensors (input devices), see Figure 10.1. These sensors can be those which detect things happening in the environment, changes in temperature, light conditions, movement, etc. The control unit can be programmed to switch on or off motors, lights and alarms according to signals received from these sensors (input devices.)

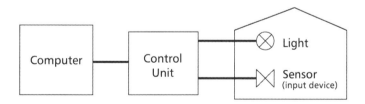

Figure 10.1. Control units with input devices

Within control technology in the ICT National Curriculum, children will learn that it is possible to attach lights, motors, buzzers or input devices to a control unit. Using the computer and the control unit, children should be able to produce simple procedures to turn on the lights, turn on motors or cause them to change direction, or to sound alarms. The children will also be involved in learning how to create, test, improve and refine sequences of instructions to make these things happen.

In order for children to achieve success with these elements they need to be able to use and understand simple electrical circuits. Typically they will have experimented and investigated simple series and parallel circuits involving switches, lights and motors. You, as the teacher, will need to be familiar with the control technology and associated software. Some control units use simple screen icons to represent the devices that are attached. Most also operate using a form of binary procedures; pupils will need to be familiar with the on/off, yes/no nature of binary language. They should also have had experience working with decision trees. Pupils will also need to be familiar with using stylised control language to control the computer's actions; typically these are similar to Logo procedures. These will be discussed in Chapter 11.

A wide range of control units is available from, for example, Deltronics Interfaces, Data Harvest and Valiant Roamer.

Foundation Stage

From the Curriculum Guidance for the Foundation Stage and the National Curriculum needs for Key Stage I, it is possible to develop a range of key skills for each year group in school. For reception the expectation would be that children are:

- **introduced to the vocabulary and language of control;**
- **aware that control technology is used in fridges, washing machines, toasters, televisions, etc;**
- **able to discuss how control technology helps them;**
- **able to use a simple programmable toy.**

Much of the initial exposure to control technology in the Foundation Stage will be through discussion of the children's experiences. The following example illustrates this point.

Teaching example 10.1

Nursery/reception

ICT learning intention: to identify objects which use technology.

Mathematical development learning intention: to sort into two discrete sets.

The teacher laminated two sets of pictures, for example:

- toaster, video recorder, cassette player, kettle, washing machine, iron, digital alarm clock;
- football, desk, loaf of bread, pram, tree, chair, puppy.

The pictures were mixed and the teacher discussed each one in turn. Then a group of children worked together with a Teaching Assistant to sort the pictures into two sets. The intention was to identify those pictures which represented technological mechanism and separate them from the rest of the group. However, whatever criteria the children chose to sort the pictures was valued, and used as the basis of discussions.

After all the children had sorted the pictures, the teacher encouraged a class discussion of how the cards had been sorted. At this stage, the teacher was able to promote the concept that some technological mechanisms have automatic features. For example, the kettle will automatically turn itself off when the water boils.

Practical task

Can you devise a different activity which would fulfil the same ICT learning intention for children in the Foundation Stage?

Clearly, within the Foundation Stage, most effective learning about technology will involve discussion around first-hand experiences. However, a practical starting point for control could be directing the movements of other pupils in the class; pupils acting as robots whose movements are directed by others. Using language such as forwards, backwards, left and right the children are learning that agreement, precision and clarity are need for instructions to work. Elements of this can often be undertaken during PE sessions or when children are working in the outdoor environment. However, it is important to give the work a 'meaningful' context. Pupils could be involved in moving Goldilocks around the Three Bears' House using small world equipment, again controlling the movement using directional language. Here the teacher would need to be available to intervene and direct as necessary.

Practical task

When you are next on school placement, think about how you could build these initial stages of control technology into the six areas of learning.

Key Stage I

From the National Curriculum requirements for Key Stage I it is possible to develop a range of key skills for each year group in school.

At Year I pupils should:

- **use the vocabulary and language associated with control technology;**
- **be developing independence in the use of a floor robot.**

At Year 2, pupils should:

- **be developing their use of the vocabulary and language associated with control technology;**
- **give direct commands and be able to predict the results;**
- **record a series of commands for someone else to follow.**

This next Teaching example demonstrates the Year I emphasis on effective use of language skills. It also clearly builds upon the skills, knowledge and understanding which children will have developed in the Foundation Stage. The teacher designed this activity as an adaptation of an element from the QCA Scheme of Work for ICT (Unit IF: Understanding Instructions and Making Things Happen).

Teaching example 10.2

Year 1

ICT learning intention: to formulate a series of clear and precise instructions.

English speaking and listening learning intention: to give and follow a sequence of simple instructions; to understand the need for clarity with instructions.

The teacher created a number of large labels or pictures to represent the parts of a 'treasure island'; sandy beach, palm trees, treasure box, pirate's house, for example. The teacher told the children they were going to be explorers searching the island. She discussed the different places on the island and helped them to label areas around the room to indicate places on the island.

One child was chosen to be the explorer. The teacher chose an island location at random, and the rest of the class took it in turns to offer suitable instructions such as forward four steps, right turn, forward eight steps, left turn, etc, so that the child could locate the specified place on the island. This was repeated with different children acting as the explorer.

Reflective task

What support would be needed for children not sure of left and right?

What discussions might you need to have regarding the children's movements such as length of pace and accuracy of turning right angles?

The teacher had planned to extend the above work and add a clearer mathematical context, by enabling the children to develop their instructions to include more precise units of measurement. The progression has been emboldened in the learning intentions, below.

Teaching example 10.3

Year 1

ICT learning intention: to formulate a series of clear and precise instructions **using measurable units**.

Mathematical learning intention: to give a sequence of instructions **using measurable units** and the terms forwards, backwards, right and left.

The teacher used a large map drawn on squared paper, and a small world character. She pointed out how the square grid divided the map into separate elements, and then demonstrated how to lead the explorer around the map. She modelled a route the explorer might take, writing out the moves, for example:

- forward three squares;
- left turn;
- forward two squares;
- right turn.

Then, working in pairs, the children led the explorer on their own plans; moving him, for example, from the beach to the pirate's house.

At the end of the session the teacher asked the children to demonstrate on the class map some of the routes they had created.

As an extension activity the teacher provided a chart for the more able children to predict the instructions a Roamer (floor robot) would need to make any particular journey.

Reflective task

How can you ensure that the children realise that right and left are commands to turn and not moves sideways?

The teacher had provided extension work for the more able children. Consider how you would support any less able children with this type of activity.

Once the children are familiar with using control-type language they will be able to experience using and working with a floor robot. This activity introduces the idea of programming a floor turtle to move around an area using single instructions. When working with programmable toys pupils are continuing to develop their spatial skills; the focus is the concept that accurate control requires a series of accurate instructions.

Up to this point the pupils have been giving directions to other pupils. Forward and backward are generally unproblematic terms, although the issue of different stride length can pose an interesting starting point for discussion. This is useful since it can lead into the concept of using standard units. This point was made in Teaching example 10.3. It also offers a useful link to the developing need for a standard unit in measures.

There is a related issue, however, that is a little more complex: the notion of measuring a turn. The instructions have been for the pupils to make a 'right turn' or 'left turn'. The teacher in the examples illustrated these turns by demonstrating a quarter turn, or right angle. When instructing each other, this does not pose a problem. However, floor robots have a number of different ways of dealing with the issue of the 'right angle'. The Roamer, by default, requires the amount of turn to be given in degrees. Pupils working with a Roamer to turn a 'quarter turn to the right' will therefore be giving the floor robot the instruction to turn right 90°. This may well be a larger number than the pupils have worked with before. Because of this, it is possible to adapt most floor robots' settings so that the degrees are not used. However, this could lead to yet more misunderstandings, and the majority of teachers who use the Roamer tend to leave the setting as it is. Pupils will be meeting the concept of degrees as a 'measure of turn' later in their school life. Although the full concept of the measurement is complex for young children to grasp and at this stage they may not fully comprehend it, it is still useful for them to experience the language.

The following activity was designed to further develop the pupils' knowledge and understanding of both the control language and the use of accurate measurement. The theme was space exploration; knowledge of our solar system and the planets is not an element within the Key Stage 1 National Curriculum. However, the context is motivational and is used for that purpose. The main learning is clearly focused on the control aspect of ICT.

Teaching example 10.4

Year 2
ICT learning intention: to program a floor robot (Roamer) using the commands forward, backward, right and left, so that it follows a desired path.

Science learning intention: to recognise and name the nine planets of our solar system.

Inspired by a book from the reading scheme, the pupils had been discussing space and the planets of the solar system. Groups of pupils had produced paintings and the teacher decided to use this interest to facilitate learning in ICT. In an open area the teacher temporarily fixed the pupils' paintings of the planets to the floor. She explained that the Roamer is a rocket ship; reminded them about their previous work on directional instructions, and discussed the instructions that the Roamer uses. She showed the pupils how to enter instructions, and to press 'Go' to start it moving.

The teacher then explained that they would be astronauts leaving Earth and arriving on Neptune. The pupils will have to instruct the Roamer rocket to travel to a specific planet. She let the group experiment with the command, and encouraged them to predict the kind of instruction they would need to make it reach Neptune.

The pupils had task sheets which involved them navigating from one planet to another, recording the sequences of instructions needed for a trip.

Reflective task

On your last school experience were there any opportunities where you could have capitalised on the pupils' interests to direct your teaching?

If on your next school placement you have access to a desktop programmable robot (like a Pixie or a mini Roamer) this type of work can be undertaken in the corner of most classrooms. However, normal floor robots will require large amounts of space. If this is only available outside the teaching area then this type of activity may need to be undertaken when additional adult help is available.

There are many other activities that will enable pupils to practise entering instructions into a floor robot.

- **On target. A circle is marked on the floor some distance from the floor robot, the pupils enter commands so that the robot moves forward and stops in the target area. The pupils are encouraged to use trial and improvement methods to adapt their instructions until they can get the robot exactly in the centre of the target.**
- **Hit the skittles. The robot is placed some distance away from a group of playground skittles; the children have to enter a series of commands so the robot drives forward and knocks over as many skittles as possible.**
- **Slalom. A series of cones or other markers are placed at intervals in a line. The pupils have to program the robot so that it will navigate the route, following a zig-zag or castellated route.**
- **A floor robot as a postman. The robot is programmed to move along the floor and stop at predetermined locations to 'deliver letters', waiting for a few seconds and then continuing along the journey.**
- **Sheepdog. The pupils place 'sheep' models in a large open area, an open box or pen area is marked on the floor. The pupils then program the floor robot to explore the area, pushing sheep towards the pen.**
- **Lost in a maze. The floor robot is surrounded by a maze of block play equipment and the children have to enter commands so that the robot can safely manoeuvre itself to the exit.**

With these and other ideas, it is important to encourage the pupils to think carefully and to plan the sequences of commands before they start entering instructions. It is also useful to give the pupils a written sequence of commands and ask them to predict what actions they think the sequence will cause the floor robot to perform. A related idea is to offer the children a sequence of instructions containing a number of errors; the pupils work together to check the commands and correct them.

Practical task

Make a note of any other control activities you can develop using a floor robot. Are there any with clear cross-curricular links?

The essence of control technology is the children's ability and confidence to use technological methods to control real events and objects. This section has illustrated a number of easy ways of doing that using programmable robots for Key Stage I. The knowledge, skills and understanding, and much of the language children develop using floor robots, lead into using the computer language Logo. This will be considered in more detail in Chapter II.

To develop the pupil's capabilities with the use of control language, they can also use software simulations such as Roamer World or The Crystal Rainforest. These applications offer the option of practising control language at different levels of difficulty and within various contexts. They are valuable, flexible educational tools when used to develop modelling or exploration skills. However, they do not completely fulfil the requirement for control, since they rely upon controlling screen elements and not real objects or events.

Key Stage 2

As with the earlier Key Stage, it is possible to break the ICT National Curriculum requirements for Key Stage 2 into a series of developmental stages.

For Years 3 and 4 pupils should:

- **discuss the use of control technology in everyday life;**
- **offer direct instructions to control a range of devices ;**
- **be able to use simple control units to operate a model;**
- **be able to use simple sensors for monitoring conditions (changes in temperature or sound levels, for example).**

For Years 5 and 6, pupils should:

- **confidently use control units to control a range of events;**
- **write and edit procedures to control a series of events;**
- **use sensing equipment to monitor a range of conditions.**

It is clear from these points that during this Key Stage pupils will be taught to control a greater range of devices. By the end of Year 6 they will be able to use control units to control a number of simple devices. Initially, this work will utilise direct instructions, where the devices respond to each individual command. A control unit, for example, can be given direct commands which are turned into immediate actions. For example, children giving a 'switch on motor I' command and the control unit would automatically operate a switch to connect the circuit to motor I.

Later these commands will become sequences of commands, a program or a procedure which will control a sequence of events. Control units often use computer software to enable children to quickly design a set of instructions to be carried out in sequence. This is a program, or procedure. A simple program could, for example, switch on a light, wait for 60 seconds before switching the light off again and switching on a second light. Using a number of lights and sequences of instructions children can use this facility to emulate a traffic light system.

Although many control units need to be linked to a computer, some units offer simplified control without the use of a computer or additional software. Such units include, for example, Learn & Go from Data Harvest. Learn & Go provides a clear first step towards control without a computer. It enables the children to advance from working with simple electrical circuits to programming a sequence of on–off switch procedures.

Figure 10.2. Learn & Go

In the following Teaching example, the project was to build a model working a simplified traffic-light system with three lights controlled using a Learn & Go control unit. The children created a series of instructions, tested them and then modified them where necessary.

Teaching example 10.5

Year 3
ICT learning intention: to use control technology to automatically control a series of linked events.

PSHE learning intention: to identify what the rules of the road are and how they are enforced.

As part of a topic linked to the local environment and road safety the class was focusing on personal, social and health education (PSHE), in particular preparing to play an active role as citizens. This involved the class in discussions as to why and how rules and laws are made and enforced, with particular emphasis on 'rules of the road'.

The children were encouraged to duplicate a traffic light system. They were then given time to experiment with a set of lights and batteries. They produced simple circuits to make the three lights work and were able to simulate a working traffic light by manually operating a set of switches.

Then the group were introduced to the Learn & Go control unit that they would need to use. The teacher demonstrated the use of the connections and the buttons.

The next stage was to connect the existing circuits to the control unit. A Teaching Assistant helped the children to disassemble their switches and to connect their circuits appropriately. The children made careful note of the connections so that they would be able to write a suitable series of commands to operate the lights. The children were then encouraged to write their program in words. Using the Learn & Go unit meant that the children could write a control script in English:

Red light on   Wait 10 seconds
Red light off

Amber light on   Wait 10 seconds
Amber light off

Green light on   Wait 10 seconds
Green light off

The children ensured that the lights were correctly connected to the control unit and then performed the 'script' once using the Learn & Go buttons. This programmed the control unit so that it could repeat the procedure automatically.

After running the program the children were encouraged to discuss what had happened and to share any problems. They then considered ways of developing or improving their script.

Reflective task

What kind of problems do you think children could encounter when working on projects such as this?

Is it always advisable to anticipate and prevent difficulties arising or should children be allowed to encounter issues as part of a teaching strategy?

This teaching example used a control unit that did not require it to be linked to a computer or software. However, many control units are available which work in tandem with a computer. The software with these units will enable pupils to use a more sophisticated series of commands. Logo's ROBOLAB, for example, uses an icon-based program to enable children to quickly write programs to control a number of devices. The control software has a range of programming options that allow the programming level to match the pupils' level of knowledge and skills. This usually means that the pupils can work through a progressive series of structured tasks, working from starting and stopping a motor, through using touch sensors and light sensors to programming a number of devices through multiple steps. Systems like this clearly offer a great deal of support. There can be a drawback however, in that until they have progressed through the early stages, children's creativity and ingenuity can be stifled by the closed systems. Once children have gained the confidence and skills necessary, however, it may be more useful to allow them time to explore more open-ended problems.

The following Teaching example illustrates how one teacher worked with a Year 5/6 class in a way that promoted motivation and interest. The activity was focused on designing and testing a set of computer controlled systems within a shop.

Teaching example 10.6

Year 5
ICT learning intention: to use control technology to automatically control a series of linked events.

Design technology learning intention: to use electrical circuits and control technology to achieve results that work.

The class had been looking at the commercial businesses in the local environment. As part of design technology they began to think about different ways in which technology could be used to enhance shop security. The children worked in groups to identify possible security solutions. The teacher reminded the pupils about the different devices they had used with computer control units in earlier lessons. They were then encouraged to develop a design which would utilise the devices that were available. Each group decided to design and construct a particular security device. These were:

• a door alarm using a pressure pad and a buzzer;
• an automatic floodlight using a light sensor and series of bulbs;
• anti-theft devices using reed switches, pressure pads and a buzzer;
• motor driven security shutters that close automatically.

The teacher gave each group a control unit and the devices they needed for their part of the project. The children had opportunities to see how the control unit connects to the individual devices, and there was time for them to experiment and become familiar with the workings of the control software.

Each group wrote a series of instructions to make their security devices work and then tested these with the control unit. As part of these tests the pupils were encouraged to record the ways in which the devices operated; to state whether they worked the way they expected, and to record any changes they would need to make to the sequence of instructions. The process relied very strongly on trial and improvement methods. Some groups achieved success relatively quickly, others needed additional opportunities to refine and improve their commands. The teacher encouraged the pupils to share their experiences throughout the process.

As can be seen from the previous Teaching example, design technology can be closely linked, in a cross-curricular manner, to the use and exploration of control technology. Here the use of ICT can significantly enhance pupils' learning, since it directly enables them to control electrical or mechanical models they have designed and constructed. For example, pupils have successfully utilised control technology within D&T, in the following ways.

- A project related to fairground rides resulted in the pupils creating simple rotating models; the addition of control technology enabled the models to move realistically.

- A literacy project on Ted Hughes' *The Iron Man* resulted in pupils constructing a box model of the iron man; the addition of control technology enabled the model to have flashing eyes.

- A project related to supermarkets involved pupils in designing packaging, the addition of control technology enabled them to add security features.

- Work related to a museum exhibit involved the pupils making their own artefacts; the addition of control technology enabled them to create pressure sensitive switches that caused an alarm to sound when an artefact was moved.

- A project on the Egyptians encouraged pupils to design a model of a treasure room in an Egyptian tomb; using control technology the pupils created a series of sliding blocks that automatically sealed the chamber if movement was detected inside.

Control technology in practice:

a summary of key points

- *In the early years pupils need to learn that control technology is all around us and helps us in our everyday lives.*
- *There are strong links between the use of control technology and design technology.*
- *Control technology can be most successfully implemented into teaching in the primary classroom using cross-curricular approaches.*
- *There is a distinct and clear set of progressive skills to be considered when planning work using control technology.*

References

Fleming, N. D. (2001) *Teaching and learning styles: VARK strategies.* Honolulu: VARK-Learn Publications.

QCA (1998) *A scheme of work for Key Stages 1 and 2: information technology.* London: QCA Publications.

QCA (2000) *Curriculum guidance for the Foundation Stage.* London: QCA.

QCA (2005) *Information and communication technology. 2004/5 annual report on curriculum and assessment.* London: QCA.

Further reading

Pritchard, A. (2005) *Ways of learning: learning theories and learning styles in the classroom.* London: David Fulton. A detailed introduction to many of the major theories that lie behind children's learning styles. The book examines how to develop learning situations, and how to plan and create the best opportunities for effective and lasting learning.

Resources

Learn & Go from Data Harvest. Further information from www.data-harvest. co.uk/control/primary.html.

Roamer from Valiant Technology. www.valiant-technology.com/.

Pixie from Swallow Systems Ltd. Further details from www.swallow.co.uk.

Deltronics Interfaces. Further details from www.deltronics.co.uk/cinterfaces.shtml.

Robolab is part of Logo Mindstorms. Further information from www.logo.com/ education/.

11 ICT STRATEGIES: CONTROL TECHNOLOGY

By the end of this chapter you should:

- **have knowledge and understanding of the requirements for control and modelling within the ICT NC Programme of Study and ICT within the Curriculum Guidance for the Foundation Stage;**
- **recognise the ways in which control and modelling strategies can be introduced and developed in the primary classroom;**
- **be able to plan and organise learning in clearly structured, creative ways to enable children to use control and modelling technologies;**
- **be able to Identify issues of health and safety in ICT.**

Professional Standards for QTS
Q2.1, Q2.2, Q2.3, Q2.6, Q2.7, Q3.2, Q3.3, Q3.4, Q3.5

Links to the Foundation Stage Guidance and the National Curriculum

In the Foundation Stage children will use information communication technology to support their learning.

At Key Stage 1 children will plan and give instructions to make things happen, try things out and explore what happens in real and imaginary situations (2c, 2d).

At Key Stage 2 children will create, test, improve and refine sequences of instructions to make things happen, and to monitor events and respond to them. They will also use simulations and explore models in order to answer 'what if?' type questions, to investigate and evaluate the effect of changing values and to identify patterns and relationships (2b, 2c).

Introduction

> *The curriculum should use technology to extend and enhance learning. ICT is a tool for thinking and doing as well as for presenting information. The curriculum should develop learners who are confident in using ICT tools for research, analysis, creativity and communication.* (QCA 2005, p6–7)

The above quotation from the QCA's document *A Curriculum for the Future: Subjects Consider the Challenge* indicates the strong intention that pupils should use ICT in creative, open-ended ways.

The use of control technology is similar to multimedia authoring in that pupils can utilise the applications in quite creative ways. Their learning is enhanced and cross-curricular links are reinforced in a practical and engaging way.

As has been discussed in the previous chapter, the Curriculum Guidance for the Foundation Stage indicates that this creative yet practical use should start with the youngest children. The ELG make it clear that children should be involved in finding out about identifying the ways in which everyday technology helps us. There are also specific ELG that indicate that young children should *use information communication technology to support their learning* (QCA, 2000, p92). Much of this work for Foundation Stage pupils may involve children using remote control cars, recording sounds, using floor robots, moving items around a computer screen or IWB and selecting icons to make musical sounds or to animate pictures. All of these are ways in which children may use ICT to make things happen. Moving into Key Stages I and 2, the National Curriculum expands on these with a specific strand: Developing Ideas and Making Things Happen.

In this strand pupils at Key Stage I should be taught:

2c how to plan and give instructions to make things happen;

2d to try things out and explore what happens in real and imaginary situations.

Key Stage 2 pupils should be taught:

2b how to create, test, improve and refine sequences of instructions to make things happen and to monitor events and respond to them;

2c to use simulations and explore models in order to answer 'what if...?' questions, to investigate and evaluate the effects of changing values and to identify patterns and relationships.

The above elements of the National Curriculum for ICT identify ways in which pupils are involved in using control technology. The statements, *give instructions to make things happen* or *improve and refine sequences of instructions* are solely directed at the use of ICT as a tool for controlling.

Similarly, the statements *try things out and explore ... imaginary situations* or *use simulations and explore*, indicate areas where pupils are involved in using simulations or models.

This chapter will explore the areas of control technology, simulations and models in greater detail. It will unpick some of the Teaching examples discussed in Chapter 10, suggest ways of developing new activities and also discuss a number of important professional issues.

Tools and strategies

Control technology

A number of the Teaching examples from Chapter 10 illustrated ways in which control technology could be used. When thinking of this technology it is useful to classify control systems into four types, each more complex than the preceding one, see Table 11.1.

Table 11.1. Classifications of control systems

Type of system	Real world example	Teaching example
Command systems immediately carry out commands	Remote control Radio controlled toy	Giving clear instructions to: • another pupil (Teaching example 10.2) • a floor robot (Teaching example 10.3)
Programmable systems execute stored commands	Video recorder Digital alarm clock	Programming a sequence of instructions: • using procedures with a floor robot or Logo (Teaching example 10.4) • using control units to perform a series of linked actions (Teaching example 10.5)
Sensing systems respond to external conditions	Automatic lights that switch on at dusk Doors that open automatically	Using sensing units that detect changes in temperature, light levels or sound levels and send signals back to a computer, to control a series of linked events (Teaching example 10.6) and using data logging equipment with a science context (Teaching example 2.7)
Conditional systems adjust their 'behaviour' according to external conditions	Central heating systems make 'decisions' based upon the time and the temperature of the room	A range of sensing units and control systems can be used to maintain optimal environmental conditions within a greenhouse. Moisture sensors, together with temperature sensors, detect the conditions and a computer system uses this information to make 'choices' regarding which element to adjust: opening or closing shutters, or increasing or decreasing the flow of water, for example.

The four types of systems offer an indication of the kind of knowledge, understanding and skills progression that pupils should meet. From the above, it is clear that within the primary school, pupils will be using command, programmable and sensing systems, but are unlikely to create conditional systems. However, it is important that they know that this type of system exists and how it can be identified.

COMMAND SYSTEMS

To work effectively with these pupils need to think about the notion of 'action – reaction'. They need to understand that the command they offer will be performed exactly as they word (or type) it. When working with pupils (role-playing controllable robots, for example), or when offering instructions to a floor robot, the instructions need to be specific and clear.

PROGRAMMABLE SYSTEMS

Build on the above; here the pupils will be offering a series of instructions to be 'remembered' by the device and acted upon. Again, the instructions need to be given in the correct language, with precision and in the correct order or unintended results will occur. Within these systems pupils will begin to utilise more sophisticated language (using repeat functions or procedures, for example). Also see the section on Logo, later in this chapter.

SENSING SYSTEMS

When pupils are using sensing and monitoring technologies (as in Chapters 2 and 10) they are utilising devices which extend their own senses. These can be used simply to collect data, usually within a science context. However, it is also possible to associate the sensing devices with control systems. In this way, once the system is set up, the sensing instruments give the commands that will control the devices. See Teaching example 10.6.

CONDITIONAL SYSTEMS

This is a further elaboration of a sensing system. Conditional systems use information delivered to them from a number of different sensors together with a program so that the system will function in different ways according to the sensing information (inputs) it receives. This is a further technical development which requires resources beyond those that are typically available within primary schools. However, some schools are using such long-term, resource-heavy, control projects as ways of developing their transition arrangements with Key Stage 3. Children in Year 6 begin planning and working on a project which they continue working on and complete as part of their Year 7 work.

The Teaching examples from Chapter 10 demonstrate how pupils can develop their skills with using a range of these control systems. In Key Stage 2 pupils will also be combining control technology with sensing units in order to create systems which respond to changes (sensing systems) in the environment such as a 'burglar alarm'.

Practical task

When you are planning ICT for your next school placement, consider the above Table and the Teaching examples from the last chapter. If the use of control or monitoring technology is appropriate for the pupils, identify which system they have experienced before and which techniques they are confident with. Use this information to help with your planning.

As already indicated, the use of monitoring or sensing equipment is closely aligned with the science curriculum. However, control technology also offers very clear links between ICT and design and technology (D&T). The following Table (11.2) indicates the links between the National Curriculum programmes of study for both ICT and D&T, and also provides some suggestions for possible activities.

Table 11.2. Links between ICT and D&T

	In ICT pupils will:	In D&T pupils will:	Control in practice
KS 1	Give direct signals or commands that produce a variety of outcomes; use ICT based models or simulations to explore aspects of real and imaginary situations.	Work with a range of materials and components including construction kits. Apply skills, knowledge and understanding from other subjects.	Control the movement of a turtle or use on/off control in their models; design a route for turtle to go shopping, or control the lighting in a lighthouse.
KS2	Create, test, modify and store sequences of instructions to control events. Use ICT to monitor external events. Explore the effect of changing variables.	Know how mechanisms can be used to make things move in different ways, using a range of equipment including an ICT control program. Know how electrical circuits, including those with simple switches, can be used to achieve functional results.	Design and make an animated scene or kinetic model which receives information from switches; use a control interface to design and control a sequence of events: traffic lights, car park barrier or models for fairground rides.

(Adapted from Becta, 2003)

Control technology has another strong curriculum link with mathematics; particularly if children are involved in using the programming language Logo.

Although widely regarded as a purely educational program, Logo is a version of the programming language Lisp. In school it is Logo's 'turtle graphics' capabilities which are most widely used as a way of developing children's mathematical knowledge and understanding of distance and angles. Logo was created as a way of creating a micro-world where children could experience mathematical concepts.

Logo offers pupils an extremely powerful tool with which they can develop their knowledge and understanding of mathematics, geography, language, art and control technology. It can be used as a simple command system or, when pupils have developed confidence with the Logo language, as a sophisticated programmable system.

There are many different implementations of Logo available. Crystal Rainforest features a separate Crystal Logo application which has a unique 'talking Logo' feature. This is an excellent concept, the automatic narration of the Logo commands can help pupils to focus on the important link between the written command and the action taking place on screen. Another important point here is that, after the children have become familiar with using the commands, the 'talking Logo' feature can be switched off. When pupils use Crystal Logo, and other similar applications, they will be using icons to give the Logo commands. While this is most useful as a starting point, the use of the icons limits the children's creativity since they can only use the commands on screen (see Figure 11.1).

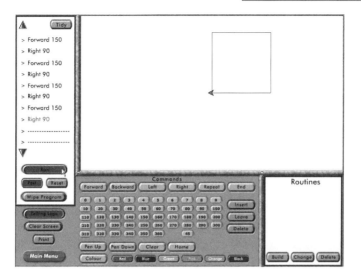

Figure 11.1. Crystal Logo image
(Reproduced by kind permission of the Sherston Publishing Group)

MSW Logo is a more powerful version of Logo. It is raw, in the sense that pupils using it will need to use the Logo language and not be able to rely on buttons or icons to drive the software. This, however, opens up more creative uses of the language for pupils who have already developed their confidence with Logo. Also, unlike other Logo implementations, MSW Logo is well supported on the internet and because it is free it can be copied for pupils to use at home.

There are some important considerations to be made when using Logo with young children; in order to discuss these some elements of the Logo language will be explored in this chapter. However, it is not the intention to offer full guidance with using Logo here. The books in the Further Reading section at the end of this chapter will offer additional guidance and suggestions.

When using most Logo implementations, the main area of the screen is the drawing area, where the turtle's movements will appear. At the bottom of the screen is the command box, where the Logo commands are written.

Logo operates on a simple logical language. Typing FORWARD 50 and pressing return will make the turtle move forward 50 steps, drawing a line as it goes. BACKWARD 25 will make the turtle back up 25 steps; it will now be in the centre of the line. RIGHT 90, or LEFT 90, will turn the turtle 90 degrees to the right or left, respectively. This is logical and easily understood. However, there are some issues.

The first of these is the size of the turtle's steps. How far is FORWARD 50? When children work with a floor robot the units are clear, and the distance the robot will move is great. Move a Roamer forward three and it covers almost a metre of ground (one Roamer step is 30cm). Move the screen turtle forward three and no one will notice it has moved. It actually moves one unit per screen pixel, and since computer screens are generally 1280 x 1024 pixels the movement is almost invisible.

This means that children will need to be familiar with using larger numbers than they did when working on the floor robot.

The second issue is the problem of right and left. With a floor robot it is relatively easy for children to follow it around, stand behind it and determine which way right or left would be. With a screen turtle, this is less clear. When the turtle is moving forwards towards the top of the screen right and left are as you would expect. However, after some movements the turtle could well be moving forwards but down the screen, now right and left have changed places. Clearly, the important notion here is for children to realise that the right and left that are important are the ones from the turtle's point of view. Young children who are struggling to remember right and left themselves, as well as being quite egocentric and having difficulties empathising with people, let alone turtles on a screen, will find this very difficult to comprehend.

The third issue revolves around the fact that for FORWARD and BACKWARD the units mean distance (small distances), but for LEFT and RIGHT the units describe the amount of turn. This was an issue with floor robots and was discussed in Chapter 10. However, at this stage, as children move through the primary years, they need to come into contact with measurements of degree, and the use of Logo will boost this understanding, so the 'problem' is actually a good opportunity to reinforce a teaching point.

Practical task

Visit the MAPE website (www.mape.org.uk) where you will be able to see a range of case studies detailing how teachers have used floor robots as part of their teaching. Identify any potential issues with the activities, and note how you could overcome them.

It is clearly helpful that pupils have a number of experiences before working with screen turtle Logo. In particular, they should have had plenty of opportunities to give, and respond to, clear 'Logo style' instructions: for example, small groups of children working in pairs. One is blindfolded and guided by their 'buddy' who offers instructions such as FORWARD 5, LEFT 90. The aim is to steer their partner to a specific spot in the hall or gym. Pupils should also have spent some time working with a floor robot to become familiar with the way in which it responds to instructions.

Then, when children start working with a screen turtle they should be reminded of their work with the floor robot. RoamerWorld from Valiant technology is a screen simulation of their Roamer, and makes this association very clear. Like Crystal Logo it is icon based, but has the option of inputting commands via the keyboard.

Screen turtles are ideally suited to drawing shapes. To create a simple shape using Logo commands, pupils will need to consider the shape's properties. For example, to construct a square they will need to use the facts that the shape has four sides, all the same length and four right angles. Having had the experiences described above, pupils will be ready to form the square using Logo language:

Forward 150
Right 90
Forward 150
Right 90
Forward 150
Right 90
Forward 150
Right 90

This list of commands produced the square in the Crystal Logo image (above), and the same commands were used for this image from MSW Logo.

Once pupils are familiar with the Logo commands they can undertake a range of other activities.

- **MSW Logo and RoamerWorld have the capability of importing an image as a background for the turtle. If an appropriate image is loaded in (of a street map of the local surroundings, for example) pupils can use Logo commands to navigate the turtle around the town.**
- **Pupils can create their own 'treasure island' image and use that as a background for the turtle to explore.**
- **Attach small sticky-notes to the computer screen and challenge the children to control the turtle so that it visits each note, or so that it moves from one side of the screen to the other avoiding all of the notes.**
- **Attach an OHP acetate to the screen and draw a simple maze on this; the children have to control the turtle around the maze.**
- **Challenge the children to draw some simple letter shapes based on right angles, such as E, F, H, I, L, T.**

The final suggestion, above, should not be seen as the beginnings of an art activity. Pupils using Logo to draw houses and ships will be frustrated in the extreme. For those activities a simple painting program will suffice. The power of Logo is its ability to follow commands and to use sequences of commands to perform specific procedures. Logo can produce effective and very artistic designs, but the learning is in the process and logical thought used to develop those designs. Pictures of houses, although a challenge to reproduce, rarely use the full programming capabilities. A better example of Logo's power is seen when pupils are asked to construct a hexagon. Again, as with the square, knowing the properties of the shape is important, pupils should realise that to make a hexagon it is necessary to make six sides and six turns. In the case of a regular hexagon, the length of each side will be the same, and the amount of each turn can be calculated by dividing 360 (the full turn in degrees) by six (the number of turns). Figure 11.2 indicates two possible solutions.

| FORWARD 70
RIGHT 60

FORWARD 70
RIGHT 60

FORWARD 70
RIGHT 60

FORWARD 70
RIGHT 60

FORWARD 70
RIGHT 60

FORWARD 70
RIGHT 60 | **The REPEAT command**

The series of instructions on the left will draw a regular hexagon. Each side is 70 units long and each turn is 60 degrees. The commands FORWARD 70 and RIGHT 60 have been grouped into pairs to show that there are in fact six separate command groups, the extra space is not necessary when using commands with Logo.

However, the list of commands is rather unwieldy and far from elegant. If children are encouraged to examine the series of commands it will become clear that in fact there is a simple pattern, the same two instructions have been repeated three times. Logo can use this repeating pattern as a short-cut. For example, the following expression, when typed into the command line of a Logo program, will produce the exact same hexagon as the list of commands.

REPEAT 6 [FORWARD 70 RIGHT 60] |

Figure 11.2. Two ways of constructing a hexagon

The solution on the left is the simple 'shopping list' of commands, which works on similar principles as the one for creating a square. The solution on the right is far more elegant, it uses Logo programming language in a more sophisticated way. The one line replaces the 12 commands. This kind of command also makes adapting the original design easier. Changing the FORWARD 70 would make a hexagon of greater or smaller size. Changing the amount of turn and the number of repeats would change the shape completely; far more powerful than having to repeatedly adjust the contents of the original list.

Later developments could be for the children to be involved in nesting repeats within repeats, creating procedures and using random numbers to further develop their understanding of the programming language. As Higgins has suggested, with Logo the pupil:

> has to engage with the mathematical nuts and bolts of the calculations to achieve their effects ... by inventing Logo procedures to create images the child is exploring their understanding of the geometric principles involved. (Higgins, 2001, p124)

The skills which children gain when they learn to successfully control elements within a computer environment are of real-life importance. However, developing those skills is not always straightforward. While some children find the challenge of using sophisticated languages like Logo stimulating and rewarding, others find it irritating. It is important to give the children a motivating and memorable context within which to work with Logo.

Practical task

Obtain a version of Logo, or download the MSW Logo version, to develop your own capabilities with this programming language.

Models and simulations

A model is a recreation of a process or series of processes. It is easier to understand the nature of 'modelling' if it is considered as having two strands:

- **structured models;**

- **unstructured models.**

Computer adventure games are generally structured models, the narrative element has been determined by the authors of the program. Within the predetermined chain of events they provide, the users will affect the way the game is played depending upon how they react to elements within it. However, there is a strong structure to the way the events will unfold. This form of a model is also known as a simulation. The Crystal Rainforest problem-solving adventure (discussed later) is a good example of this kind of model.

Some models can be designed which have no fixed structure. In this case, all elements within the model can be adapted and changed by the users. This kind of model is clearly more flexible, but is also more difficult to use. Logo falls into this category. The turtle graphics features, discussed earlier, are highly flexible, the actions model real events but there is no fixed 'narrative'.

Spreadsheet software like Excel can also be used in this highly flexible and creative way.

Most structured models (or simulation) that are widely available cover a range of ICT Programmes of Study: Ic, 2b, 2c, 4a, 4b, 4c, 5b. Schools that have adopted (or adapted) QCA Schemes of Work will find that children working with the program will rapidly work through two of the ICT units, 3D: Exploring Simulations, and 4E: Modelling Effects on Screen. The program also offers unique starting points for working directly with control equipment for QCA Units 5E (Controlling devices) and 6C (Control and Monitoring – What Happens When...?)

Clever Colin's Coffee Machine (see Figure II.3 overleaf) is an internet based model which involves pupils in making decisions regarding the amount of coffee, water, sugar and the temperature of the water to use to make the perfect cup of coffee. The model accepts a range of different inputs and will respond in particular ways until the pupils have learned the correct procedure for making the coffee.

Just Grandma & Me is a CD ROM story about a Grandma and Grandson spending a day at the seaside. One element of the story is a simple model where the pupils can design and build their own on-screen sandcastle. Another CD ROM program, Lego Loco, offers pupils an opportunity to design, build and then drive their own on-screen train sets. Models have the appeal of computer games, and the virtual world they create can be very motivating.

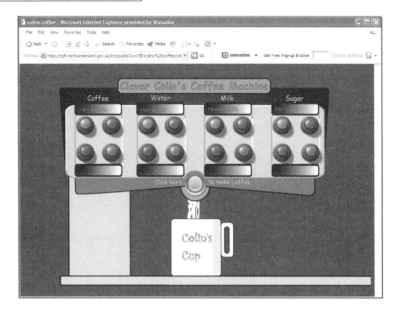

Figure 11.3. Clever Colin's Coffee Machine

More general use of models would be within the programs which are, for example, specifically designed to introduce the rudiments of composition. These programs offer children brightly coloured icons or pictograms as stand-ins for musical phrases. Software like Compose World or MusicBox 2 presents just such a graphical approach to phrasing music; children who can wield a mouse can easily use the software to create and alter sounds and melodies by 'dragging and dropping' the musical pictograms. This directly impacts their ICT knowledge, skills and understanding. By rearranging predefined musical pictograms children are trying things out and exploring what happens (2d); they are also, in a more rudimentary manner, planning and giving instructions to make things happen (2c).

Although all pupils should have the first hand experience of working with real objects (designing and building sand castles, toy train sets and musical instruments, for example) there are still valuable learning opportunities to be gained from using models. Another effective computer model is The Crystal Rainforest V2. This is an adventure story designed to introduce pupils to the use of Logo programming. The story is a mini-epic narrative, designed around a series of activities set in an alien rainforest. As pupils progress through the narrative they encounter different challenges, each one introducing new Logo features. This allows them to develop their Logo skills to move, turn, estimate distances and angles, repeat patterns, use variables and build procedures.

The Crystal Rainforest also has clear cross-curricular links, as follows.

MATHEMATICS, SPATIAL ORIENTATION, AREA AND ANGLES
Several activities within the program require children to rotate shapes or to consider their size. This could be a starting point for investigating the properties of shapes or angles.

Many of the activities involve estimating, measuring or turning through specific angles. This could be a starting point for an investigation into geometry.

ENGLISH, CREATIVE AND PERSUASIVE WRITING
The story is a simple epic tale. The children could use the format of this story to write their own episodic mythology, or produce 'back-stories' for some of the characters. Alternatively, the graphics for the activities could be used as stimuli for creative writing.

The story revolves around the destruction of a rainforest. Children will be aware of the differing viewpoints of business and conservationists. Can the children find out more about deforestation and environmental issues? What kinds of persuasive writing would help others to see their point of view?

SCIENCE, RAINFORESTS
The program may offer a starting point for investigating rainforests. Where are they on the Earth, why are they important? What is the link between rainforests, greenhouse gases and global warming? Why are the rainforests being destroyed? What can we do to reduce the destruction?

DESIGN TECHNOLOGY, ROBOTS
Inside a temple in the rainforest the children have to control robots around a series of platform mazes. Children could design their own 'levels' using an art package.

GEOGRAPHY, MAP WORK
The adventure takes the form of a journey. Children could produce an 'imaginative' map of the rainforest, identifying the areas where the challenges take place. They could use geographical symbols on their map, or invent 'alien' ones to suit the rainforest world.

Spreadsheets

This section has discussed a number of published, structured, model applications. However, unstructured mathematical models can also be developed for pupils, and by pupils, using spreadsheets. The most common form is that of a shopping model. The spreadsheet offers a range of choices of items to buy and sell and the pupils can adjust the cost and quantity of the items in order to buy the required items and yet remain in budget.

With the power of using formulae in spreadsheets pupils can also create their own models to help them solve problems. The QCA Scheme of Work Unit 6B: Spreadsheet Modelling suggests that pupils should use formulae in spreadsheets to answer 'what if …?' questions, and then explore how changes in a spreadsheet affect results and identify simple rules. The integrated task for that unit is for the pupils to use formulae to help them find out the maximum area that can be included in a rectangular field of fixed perimeter. See also Teaching example 2.6.

Professional issues

Planning and organisation

Whenever you are planning to use ICT in a teaching session it is important that you are familiar with the hardware and software the children will be using. This is especially so with control and model programs, because control equipment brings with it additional elements which need to be correctly handled and modelling software offers the user so many choices. You will need to spend some time becoming familiar with the set up of any equipment and be fully confident with the software. It is also imperative that you thoroughly trial the activities you plan to use.

When planning the activities themselves, you will also need to ensure that there is good continuity between your plans and the work the children did in the past. It is important to:

- **be sure your daily and medium term planning is informed by the school's scheme of work and the ICT policy;**
- **find out about the pupils' prior learning, this could be from the class teacher or even the teacher of the previous year group;**
- **find out what the teacher's existing ICT routines and organisational procedures are;**
- **keep clear records that will enable you to track the pupils' use of each ICT application;**
- **assess and record the pupils' developing skills; ensure that the pupils themselves understand the progress they are making and, if appropriate, keep records themselves.**

Like the work pupils may undertake when working with multimedia, control or modelling activities will take a considerable amount of time. You need to be realistic about how long an activity will take. Once a control project is underway it will need time to develop. These are often long-term projects. Once the pupils are confident with the equipment, the software and the skills necessary to make the activity work, it is important to plan for them to explore problems and situations. As has been discussed in Part 5, this independence should be concerned with encouraging discussion that allows the pupils to revise and also confirm their understanding, to construct links between their learning. This is only possible where pupils have time to reflect on their work, to explore the ICT and to develop their skills and thought processes with it. This will be enhanced if pupils are given specific opportunities to discuss their ICT work with others in the class and the teacher.

When planned well, the use of ICT in this way offers pupils time and opportunities to explore situations from quite independent and creative directions. The applications offer open-ended experiences. Contrast this with a number of integrated learning systems (ILS) and computer drill programs that you may come into contact with. These are usually based on a series of exercises or tasks which are quite closed in nature, they 'drill' knowledge or facts through a range of simple activities but have a limited scope. It has also been suggested that ILS programs have *only a moderate effect on learning gains [and] … diminish teacher and pupil control* (Clements, 2000, p37).

The more flexible use of open-ended simulations and control applications offer much more potential to engage learners and to develop their skills. Clements argues that the unique potential of ICT is only really realised when:

> it is used to provide engagement with problems and projects. Programs can provide meaningful problems for students to explore, either alone or collaboratively, making decisions as they go and receiving feedback. (Clements, 2000, p38)

Health and safety

Time needs to be spent working on simulation, but you need to be aware of how much time children are spending in front of the computer screen. Eye strain can be a common problem so ensure that children take breaks away from the screen every 15 minutes or so. You may need to encourage them to undertake a short activity away from the computer. Another potential problem is concerned with the ergonomics of the room, ensure that the seats and desk height suit the age and build of the children. This can be a concern in classrooms where children are using laptops on low desks.

Practical task

On your next school placement find out from the subject leader for ICT what the school's policy is regarding health and safety when using ICT.

ICT strategies: control technology

a summary of key points

- **The National Curriculum sets out requirements for ICT regarding the knowledge and understanding which pupils should be taught.**
- **Control technologies have strong links with design technology and science.**
- **Simulation and modelling activities can be integrated across all subject areas.**
- **Logo is an extremely powerful tool which enables pupils to develop their knowledge and understanding of mathematics, geography, language, art and control technology.**
- **Modelling applications can allow children greater freedom to explore issues and solve problems more creatively.**
- **When working with control technology it is important to give the children a motivating and memorable context.**

References

Becta (2003) *Control Technology*. www.becta.org.uk/subsections/foi/documents/technology_and_education_research/control_technology.pdf

Clements, D.H. (2000) From exercises and tasks to problems and projects – Unique contributions of computers to innovative mathematics education. *The Journal of Mathematical Behaviour*, 19 (1): 9–47.

Higgins, C. (2001) Information and communication technology in D. Eyre and L. McClure *Curriculum provision for the gifted and talented in the primary school: English, maths, science and ICT*. London: NACE-Fulton Publication.

QCA (2005) *A curriculum for the future: subjects consider the challenge*. London: QCA.

QCA (2000) *Curriculum guidance for the Foundation Stage*. London: QCA.

Further reading

Abelson, H. (1982) *Apple Logo*. Ohio: BYTE-McGraw Hill. A practical, easy to follow text which explores turtle geometry and related concepts in great detail.

Koss, M. (nd) An introduction to Logo. http://mckoss.com/logo/.

Watt, M. and Watt, D. (1986) *Teaching with Logo*. Massachusetts: Addison-Wesley. This book features a clear rationale for the use of Logo in the classroom, and a comprehensive range of ideas and strategies for teaching Logo.

QCA *Teacher's guide for information and communication technology*. Exemplifies integrated tasks from the QCA teacher's guide for information and communication technology. Available from: www.standards.dfes.gov.uk/schemes.

Resources

Clever Colin's Coffee Machine from Northumberland LA. Further information from ngfl.northumberland.gov.uk/ict/qca/ks2/unit3D/colins%20coffee/colins%20coffee.html.

Compose World 2 from Expressive Software Projects (ESP). Further details from www.espmusic.co.uk.

The Crystal Rainforest V2 from Sherston. Further details from www.sherston.com.

Just Grandma & Me published by Broderbund. Further details from www.taglearning.com.

Lego Loco from Focus Multimedia Ltd. Further details from www.focusmm.co.uk.

MSW Logo is a powerful version of Logo. It is freely available, together with additional lesson ideas and excellent support information, from www.softronix.com/logo.html.

MusicBox2 from Topologica. Further details from www.topologica.co.uk.

Pixie and Pip from Swallow. The web site includes information and ideas for integrating the use of floor robots throughout the curriculum. Further information from www.swallow.co.uk/index.htm.

Roamer and **RoamerWorld** from Valiant Technology. The web site offers an excellent range of classroom examples, ideas and resources to support all areas of the curriculum. www.valiant-technology.com/.

Textease Turtle CT offers three levels of screen interface to allow for progression. Further details available from http://www.softease.com/turtle/.

Terrapin Logo V2 from Sherston offers Logo graphics with a very user-friendly interface. Further details available from http://www2.sherston.com/.

INDEX OF TEACHING EXAMPLES

Teaching examples	ICT learning intention, to:	Context	Subject learning intention, to:	Year group
2.1	learn that technology can help gather information; to use a digital camera	Mathematical development	identify and name simple 2D shapes (squares, rectangles, circles, triangles) in the environment	R
2.2	use a digital microscope to magnify, examine and capture still and moving images	Science	identify differences between, and make comparisons of, minibeasts	Y1
2.3	use the navigation and search features of a CD ROM encyclopaedia	Music	identify key features of a range of musical instruments	Y2
2.4	use a concept planning tool to organise and share information	History	identify the reasons why the Vikings invaded and settled in Britain	Y3
2.5	use a database program and to check specific information for accuracy and to correct any implausible data	Geography	use appropriate geographical vocabulary	Y5
2.6	use formulae in a spreadsheet program to solve mathematical problems	Mathematics	approach and work through problem solving tasks systematically	Y6
2.7	use ICT data logging equipment to collect temperature data over a period of time	Science	use line graphs to show continuously changing data	Y4
4.1	control a mouse pointer to 'click and drag' a screen element	Mathematical development	recognise and read the names of the colours	R
4.2	locate and use specific letter keys and the 'enter' key	Literacy	be confident reading and writing C-V-C words	Y1
4.3	none	Literacy	use base joins, in a joined handwriting style	Y3
4.4	use concept mapping software to organise their ideas	History	identify the chain of events following the start of the fire	Y3
4.5	combine text and graphics in order to convey information in a meaningful way	Geography	use geographical vocabulary to label familiar features; eg: hill, valley, river, road, motorway, lake, road	Y2
4.6	learn that email is a quick method of communicating with wider audiences	Literacy	use appropriate conventions when writing for a specific audience	Y3
6.1	drag objects using an IWB	Mathematical development	name and sort simple 2D shapes: square, triangle, and circle	N
6.2	use ICT to model the construction of a simple circuit using images and text	Science	design and label circuit diagrams using a range of lights, batteries, switches, buzzers and connectors	Y3
6.3	use a mouse to select screen elements	KUW	find out about, and identify, some features of living things	N
6.4	use a mouse to accurately select screen elements and buttons	Mathematical development	recognise numerals 1–9	R
6.5	use the conventions of a talking book	Literacy	identify the left–right convention of the written word	Y1

Teaching examples	ICT learning intention, to:	Context	Subject learning intention, to:	Year group
6.6	use a mouse to accurately select screen elements and buttons	Creative development – music	create a simple sound sequence	R
6.7	use presentation software to create a linear multimedia book	Literacy	write for a specific audience	Y5
6.8	use hyperlinks to create a presentation using parent–child pages	History	identify the main features in a Roman settlement	Y4/5
6.9	use a web authoring package to create a series of linked pages as part of the school's web site	Geography	identify and describe the main features of Whitby town	Y6
8.1	to accurately use the mouse to select screen icons	Literacy	read and recognise initial and final phonemes in C-V-C words	R
8.2	use 'click and drag' to move icons into selected positions	Creative development – art	create a simple repeating pattern	R
8.3	work collaboratively to use a graphical modelling program to explore alternative design ideas	Design technology	use their own experience to generate new ideas to satisfy specific criteria	Y2
8.4	develop and refine ideas by creating and reorganising text	Literacy	use alliteration as the structure for a poem	Y4
8.5	work with others to explore a variety of alternative designs using a graphical modelling program	Mathematics	use addition and subtraction to solve real life problems	Y5
10.1	identify objects which use technology	Mathematical development	sort into two discrete sets	N/R
10.2	formulate a series of clear and precise instructions	English speaking and listening	give and follow a sequence of simple instructions; to understand the need for clarity with instructions	Y1
10.3	formulate a series of clear and precise instructions using measurable units	Mathematics	give a sequence of instructions using measurable units and the terms forwards, backwards, right and left	Y1
10.4	program a floor robot (Roamer) using the commands forward, backward, right and left, so that it follows a desired path	Science	recognise and name the nine planets of our Solar System	Y2
10.5	use control technology to automatically control a series of linked events	PSHE	identify what the rules of the road are and how they are enforced	Y3
10.6	use control technology to automatically control a series of linked events	Design technology	use electrical circuits and control technology to achieve results that work	Y5

This glossary contains most of the technical items mentioned throughout the text of this book, together with a selection of other useful acronyms and terms. Clearly it is only a starting point. If you wish to learn further technical expressions, an efficient method is to use an Internet search engine.

Applet A small self-contained application which can run on its own or inside another program (eg a web browser).

Attachment A file attached to email in the format it was created in, useful for documents and graphics in particular.

Bandwidth The amount of stretch in a network connection – its maximum carrying capacity for data.

Binary A file in pure data form.

Bit A binary unit.

Bmp Bitmap. A graphics file.

Bps Bits per second. Measurement of data movement through a modem, also Kbps (Kilobits per second) and Mbps for megabits per second.

Broadband A high bandwidth network, greater than 256Kbps.

Cache Small memory store for regularly accessed or recently used data.

Client An individual's computer and the program it uses to request information from a server computer/program.

Compression Making a file smaller by removing all the bits it doesn't need for faster transfer and/or storage.

Cookie A packet of data stored on your hard drive by a web site, which is sent back to the web server when information is required.

Domain A part of the address hierarchy a machine is placed in; e.g. bbc.co.uk is 'bbc' in the co.uk (company in UK) domain

Download Loading information from another computer into your own; the opposite is upload.

DTP Desktop publishing software. Formatting a document on a computer screen with an accurate representation of the printed version. See WYSIWYG.

Emoticons Portmanteau of 'emotion(al) icon'. Light-hearted term for the small text-based symbols inserted into emails and text messages, such as the familiar smiley :-) :-/

Encryption Method of coding data so that it can only be read by specific people.

F2F Face-to-face. Pertains to communication situations usually without computers where people speak personally to each other.

FAQ Frequently asked questions.

Firewall Network hardware and software that limits access between an internal network and the rest of the internet.

Flame A message that 'burns' the person it is directed at, mostly publicly. Often random and pointless, especially in newsgroups.

Freeware Software and utilities made freely available. Although no fees are paid, the freeware is still covered by copyright.

FTP File transfer protocol. System for moving files across networks.

GIF Graphics interchange format – for storing and exchanging pictures.

GUI Graphical user interface.

Hotspot A touch-sensitive part of an image on a web page linking it to another page or site.

HTML Hypertext markup language. The tags used to prepare information for web pages, including text and links.

HTTP Hypertext transfer protocol. The communications protocol that enables web browsing.

Hyperlink A touch-sensitive area or icon on a web page linking it to another page or site.

Hypertext Text that includes hyperlinks to other documents.

ISDN Integrated services digital network. Uses existing phone lines and computer networks to deliver fairly fast video, voice and data in standard form.

ISP Internet service provider.

IWB Interactive white board.

Java A programming language used to write java applets.

JPEG Joint Photographic Experts Group. An image compression and display method; quality varies as some files can be reduced by up to 20x their original size.

LAN Local area network. The cable connection between two or more computers.

Macro A macro is an abbreviation for a set of commands, or a procedure. Instead of typing a complicated sequence of commands you can use the macro's name.

Mailing list A list of subscribers to a discussion group, who all receive the discussion by mail; also used as a way of distributing newsletters.

MIDI Musical instrument digital interface. A standard protocol for synthesizers and computers to communicate, enabling musicians to compose on the synth keyboard and save the music information on the computer for manipulation in score writing programs.

MIME Multipurpose internet mail extensions. An internet standard for transferring sound and pictures by email.

Model A recreation of a process or series of processes.

Modem Modulator/demodulator – a device that converts digital signals to analogue (and vice versa), thus allowing transmission of data.

Moderator Ensures all contributions to a newsgroup are suitable before posting them.

MP3 MPEG-3 – an audio compression algorithm.

MPEG Motion picture expert group. Standard for encoding/decoding digital video.

Netiquette The unofficial rules for defining proper behaviour on the internet.

Newbie A pejorative term for beginners on the net.

Newsgroup A discussion group on a specific topic. Part of Usenet.

Plug-In An add-on feature for your browser that increases functionality, such as providing multimedia capabilities.

POS Programmes of study.

Protocol A set of procedures for establishing and controlling data transmission.

RAM Random access memory.

ROM Read-only memory.

Root directory The uppermost directory of a collection of files.

Router A device used to transfer packets from a computer on one network (LAN) to other computers on other networks via the fastest and most efficient route.

Search engine A program that searches indexes of addresses using keywords. The depth of the search is up to you and/or the extent of its index.

Server Any computer that stores information and makes it available to outside users.

Shareware Copyright-protected software that is publicly distributed on the condition that if a user trials a program and decides to keep using it they will send payment to the author.

SMTP Simple mail transport protocol. A transfer method for mail on the net.

Spam Unsolicited advertising sent via email or posted to a newsgroup. Repeat spammers are often flamed.

Streaming A method of delivering data in a steady flow to perform a task 'live', such as playing sounds or tracking action in a networked game.

TIFF Tagged image file format. Common graphics file format for still images.

URL Uniform resource locator. The address system used on the web.

Usenet The network of discussion groups or newsgroups.

WAN Wide area network. A group of computers separated by great distances but joined by dedicated lines.

WYSIWYG What you see is what you get. The capability of a computer application to accurately represent the printed document on screen.

Zip Software files compressed into ZIP format. A convenient method of packaging files for internet delivery. Generally, the zipped file must be unzipped before use with tools like WinZip or PK Zip.

2connect, 25, 37, 53
2D shapes, 36, 75
3D design program, 110

activity relevance, 121
animation, 96–97, 100
  teaching timeframe, 97
area and angles, 154

Becta, 35, 55

CD ROM encyclopaedia, 24, 57
CD ROM, 22, 23, 39, 53, 93, 95, 101, 153
Clicker 5, 50
clusters, 9
collaborative work, 122–124, 127
computers
  clusters, 9
  mobile, 9, 10
  suite, 9
  touch sensisitve screen, 41
concept keyboards, 40
concept mapping, 25, 52
control systems
  classifications, 146
  command, 146
  conditional, 146, 147
  programmable, 146, 147
  sensing, 146, 147
control technology, 130
control unit, 139, 140
Crocodile Clip, 77
Crystal Rainforest, 39, 148, 153, 154
curriculum planning, ICT, 11
cyberbullying, 70

data logging, 28–29
database, branching, 35, 37
decision trees, 34
desk top publishing, 55, 64
dictionary, talking, 53
digital camera, 18, 33, 97
digital microscope, 20
digital recorder, 38
digital video, 73

digitally recorded sound, 95

EasySensor Q, 28
email, 56, 70
email, blocking, 70
e–wordsheet, 54
Excel, 26

Flash, 100
Flexitree, 34–35
floor robots, 131, 135–136, 137, 146, 149–150
FrontPage, 87

group work, 122

health and safety, 42, 70, 157
hyperlinks, 57, 83–86, 99

ICT
  control technology, 144–158
  cross–curricular links, 11, 57
  exploration, 15–30, 32–44
  exploring, 33
  Foundation Stage, 12, 16, 45, 60, 107, 132
  health and safety, 42, 70, 157
  Key Stage 1, 61, 89, 92, 110, 133, 148
  Key Stage 2, 24, 45, 61, 63, 89, 92, 112, 138, 148
  links with design & technology, 148
  monitoring and assessing, 68–69
  OFSTED, 46
  organisation and differentiation, 128
  planning and managing, 7–14, 39–40, 65, 156
  potential health risks, 42
  reading skills, 61
  science connection, 27
  special educational needs, 13, 40, 68, 80
  written communication, 46, 51
identifying technology, 16
images, 93
information
  entering, 38
  gathering, tools, 33
  retrieving, 38
  storing, 38

Intellikeys, 41
interactive white board, 41, 66, 73, 74, 75, 87, 101
internet, 23, 43
investigation process, 35

Key Stage 1 skills, 62
Key Stage 2 skills, 63
keyboards
  concept, 40, 50, 62
  early years, 49, 60
  onscreen, 50
  sizes, 41

Learn & Go unit, 139
Learning Ladder, 39
Lisp, 148
Logo, 148–152

mathematical development, 18, 26–27, 75
memory games, 53
mobile computing, 9, 10
models
  structured, 153
  unstructured, 153
mouse adapters, 41
mouse control, 48, 68, 81, 108, 121
Mouser, 41
multimedia
  learning tool, 97
  linear presentation, 82–83
  monitoring and assessing, 102
  planning and organisation, 101
  teaching tool, 100
multimedia communication, 72–88, 89–104
multimedia use
  child, 82, 91
  teacher and child, 74, 91
  teacher, 73, 91
  teacher prescribed, 78
music, 23, 95

online activity, 78
online dictionary, 57
organisation
  single computer classroom, 9
  suite or cluster computers, 9

podcasts, 73, 96
PowerPoint, 57, 64, 73, 97, 98
programming language, 148–152
pupil differentiation, 40, 68
pupil inclusion, 40, 67, 68
resources, 8
  organisation of, 8
  hardware, 8
  software, 8

reviewing, modifying and evaluating, 118–129
Roamer, 135–136
robots, floor, 131, 135–136, 137, 149–150

school internet policy, 43
school website, 67, 73, 96
self assessment, 13, 42, 103, 125–126
self–esteem, 119
sensing equipment, 28
software
  concept mapping, 25, 52
  word processing, 46, 48, 57, 64, 93
sound, 95
spatial orientation, 154
special educational needs, 13, 40, 68, 80
spelling, 53
spreadsheets, 26, 155
Starspell, 53
suite, 9
Superhighway Safety, 43

talking book, 54, 61, 64, 72
talking dictionary, 53
Textease, 79, 83, 93, 97, 98
texting, 55, 67, 70
textual communication, 45–58, 59–71
touch sensitive screen, 41
trackballs, 41

web authoring, 86, 99
webquests, 57
whole class activity, 102
word processing software, 46, 48, 64, 79, 113
Wordshark, 53